T0277658

"Daniel Denk's winsome and thoug~~h~~ in Christian life are illuminating and e........... ..~~ .. ..~~ appreciated not only in the reading but also for the lasting reminders to cultivate joy in all that one does."

— George Marsden
University of Notre Dame

"These reflections on joy are very encouraging. As Daniel Denk makes clear, we live in a world filled with sorrows, disappointments, and dangers, but joy is a gift from God; it is both a feeling and something far deeper that inhabits our very being. Listen to Denk. He knows life in its depths, he knows God, and he knows joy. May his book bring joy to many."

— Joel Carpenter
Calvin University

"In *An Invitation to Joy*, Daniel Denk invites us to rediscover and receive a joy once lost, often challenged, even absent from the lived experience at times, but available through divine intervention. This volume offers a much-needed hope for human flourishing, carefully argued but joyful to read with profound insights and practical inquiries."

— Adriaan C. Neele
Puritan Reformed Theological Seminary

"While there are books we enjoy and books we learn from, Dan Denk's *An Invitation to Joy* is both and more. It is a book I needed. And I suspect (and hope) that I won't be alone in this. A generation surfeited with would-be pleasures and awash in pain-avoiding diversions, we are nonetheless bereft of joy. But Denk shows us that joy is worthy of serious and sustained contemplation — more than that, a gift our rejoicing God wills to give us."

— Garwood P. Anderson
Nashotah House Theological Seminary

"Daniel Denk's *An Invitation to Joy: The Divine Journey to Human Flourishing* is a powerful tool in these times of tremendous sorrow and pain, a book grounded in the word of God and in all we know as the foundation of our faith in Jesus Christ. I see this book in church libraries everywhere, in Bible study classes across denominations, at theological seminars, in classrooms, and on every family shelf. This is a powerfully urgent and long-awaited book."

— **Patricia Jabbeh Wesley**
poet, academic, and author of
Praise Song for My Children: New and Selected Poems

An Invitation to Joy

The Divine Journey to Human Flourishing

Daniel J. Denk

WILLIAM B. EERDMANS PUBLISHING COMPANY
GRAND RAPIDS, MICHIGAN

Wm. B. Eerdmans Publishing Co.
4035 Park East Court SE, Grand Rapids, Michigan 49546
www.eerdmans.com

© 2023 Daniel J. Denk
Published 2023
Printed in the United States of America

29 28 27 26 25 24 23   1 2 3 4 5 6 7

ISBN 978-0-8028-8308-7

Library of Congress Cataloging-in-Publication Data

A catalog record for this book is available from the Library
of Congress.

Unless otherwise noted, Bible quotations are from the English Standard
Version (ESV).

To my children, my teachers:
Ramona, Carmen, Allison, Ransom

Contents

Foreword

I grew up in the Reformed tradition in a Presbyterian church in Belfast, Northern Ireland. It was a very serious-minded church in which the Bible was thoroughly preached and children like me thoroughly catechized in our faith. I remember learning the Shorter Catechism of the Westminster Assembly with its question, "What is the chief end of man?" (meaning, what is the ultimate point and purpose of being human), and the classic answer, "The chief end of man is to glorify God *and enjoy him forever.*" Looking back on that childhood church, I can attest that God was being glorified, but I can't say that he was being enjoyed very much. Enjoyment was not really what church was about, certainly not on the Lord's Day.

And yet, we sang the psalms every week — for many years in the unaccompanied metrical four-part harmony of the old Scottish Psalter (singing bass in the church choir as soon as my voice broke was how I came to meet the lovely girl singing soprano who has been my wife now for fifty-two years, so I can't complain). And the psalms are full of joy! Even most of the ones that are full of lament have a turn to determined joy in the midst of suffering and injustice. So, yes, we would sing the glorious One Hundredth Psalm, with this stanza:

O enter then his gates with praise,
Approach with joy his courts unto:
Praise, laud and bless his name always,
For it is seemly so to do.

But whatever was "seemly" about our "joy" took on a rather solemn demeanor under the grand, rich tones of the "Old Hundredth" doxology arrangement. In my memory now it seems that joy was something we could affirm by faith and even sing *about*, and maybe look forward to in heaven, but not intensely *feel* with genuine emotion or express with outward visible and physical celebration (or ritual, oh no, not in a Presbyterian church) in the here and now.

Later in life my wife and I found our home in the Anglican tradition of the Church of England, and I was ordained to pastoral ministry in 1977. I relish the liturgical tradition of this communion, with its deep scriptural roots in the Reformation. But I recall the sense of irony I used to have, leading Morning or Evening Prayer, when it came to the short sequence of responsive invocations all drawn from various psalms. I would intone, "Endue thy Ministers with righteousness." And the congregation would respond, with equally mournful chant, "And make thy chosen people joyful."

It must be one of the most unanswered prayers in church history, or at least one for which the Almighty has found his "chosen people" most resistant to all his attempts to answer it.

So there is indeed something of an ironic disconnect between what we say and sing in church about joy and rejoicing and our actual lived experience, whether in life in general or in corporate and personal worship in particular. That's why I welcome this lovely book by Dan Denk, which I hope you will find, as I have, refreshing, rebuking, reviving, rewarding, and richly biblical and practical. It is so, well, "enjoyable"!

I resonate personally with Dan's self-description as not naturally an outwardly "joyful" or emotionally expressive character. Temperamentally introverted, I don't intentionally *hide* my emotions; it's just that I don't easily give voice or visibility to them — but they are very much there within me! And I also resonate with Dan's testimony of a lifetime of being sustained with a substratum of inner joy that flows from simply being a child of God and knowing his saving grace, steady presence, and fatherly care along every twist and turn of life's roller coaster.

The sad irony of the absence or deficiency of joy in much Christian experience is all the more surprising when we recall that it comes second in Paul's list of the fruit of the Spirit in Galatians 5:22, sandwiched between love and peace. Indeed, Paul links those three so often that it is clear they are essential components of Christian identity and the transforming presence of God's Spirit in a human life.

Paul is particularly fond of the two words "joy" and "peace." This is the kind of thing he loves to say:

> For the kingdom of God is not a matter of eating and drinking but of righteousness and *peace and joy* in the Holy Spirit. (Rom. 14:17)

> May the God of hope fill you with all *joy and peace* in believing, so that by the power of the Holy Spirit you may abound in hope. (Rom. 15:13)

In fact, Paul speaks of joy twenty-one times and peace forty-three times in his letters! But we can see in those verses in Romans that, for Paul, joy and peace are not just incidental by-products of the Christian faith. They are not just happy feelings. Look at what else he says about them in just those two verses — it's an impressive list.

xi

- Joy and peace are key signs of the kingdom of God — just as important as righteousness. These are things that happen when God reigns — true joy and peace are born.
- Joy and peace are the way we are to serve and please God — not in solemn anxiety.
- Joy and peace are essential ingredients in our Christian hope; we are to be *filled* with joy and peace.
- Joy and peace are evidence of the power of the Holy Spirit, overflowing in our lives.

So it's not surprising that Paul includes joy and peace in the fruit of the Spirit! These words are not just describing a cheerful, contented emotional state. This is something profound and at the heart of our Christian life and witness.[1]

In giving such a prominent place to joy in believers' lives (both individually and collectively) Paul is echoing the Scriptures that he knew so well. For the fact is that joy is abundant in the vocabulary, the worship, and the experience of Old Testament Israel. We think immediately of the book of Psalms. Even in the midst of suffering, enemies, lament, and protest, the voice of joy is never far away. Celebrate, sing, rejoice, praise, give thanks, be glad . . . over and over again. A people shaped by the frequency of such worship songs must have learned something about the character and desires of the God they worshipped, if these were the praises on which he was enthroned.

Indeed, for Israel joy was not an optional "icing on the cake" of life. It was commanded! The rhythm of the year was punctuated by three week-long festivals (Unleavened Bread, Weeks, and Tabernacles; Lev. 23 and Deut. 16). Apart from the benefit of rest from work

---

1. Christopher J. H. Wright, *Cultivating the Fruit of the Spirit: Growing in Christlikeness* (Downers Grove, IL: InterVarsity Press, 2017), 37–38.

in those weeks (did you know annual holidays are biblical, as well as the weekly sabbath day off?), they were to be times of *mandatory* rejoicing and celebration. "Rejoice before the LORD your God at the place he will choose as a dwelling for his Name. . . . Be joyful at your festival" (Deut. 16:11, 14 NIV). God's abundant blessing should generate abundant joy, celebrated with festive eating and drinking. That's an order!

Celebration of harvests is a cause for joy throughout human cultures, of course. In that sense, Israel was not unique. But it is remarkable how the Old Testament links joy and thankfulness to God with a wide range of experience, from the very special (such as the magnificence of creation, the gift of God's law, the grace of forgiveness, the building of the tabernacle and later the temple, or the coronation of a new king), down to the very ordinary and mundane (daily work, sleep and rest, bread and wine, olive oil and fruit, sex, love and friendship, beauty in nature and the human form). Gratitude for all these ordinary things in life, recognized as gifts of God, is (as Israel was taught and Dan Denk will emphasize) one of the most potent engines of real and lasting joy.

Israel was taught two more things, however, that should also govern our Christian aspiration for joy-filled lives.

First, joy must be socially inclusive. Not just in the sense that it should be something we enjoy together (we all enjoy a good party or a rousing time of songs of praise), but rather in the sense that we should intentionally seek to make sure nobody is left out. In Israel, there were those who for various reasons were vulnerable and might have little cause or resources for celebration. This included those who did not have land of their own to harvest (slaves, foreigners, and the tribe of Levites) and those who had lost the family security of husbands and fathers (widows and orphans). God's instructions emphasized that all such people were to be included in the festivities: "Rejoice before the Lord your God at the place he will choose as a dwelling for his Name — you, your sons and daughters, *your male and female servants, the Levites in your towns, and the foreigners, the fatherless and the widows living among you*" (Deut. 16:11, 14 NIV; my italics). Much later on, Nehemiah may have had this in mind when he announced a day of rejoicing with an important provision. Nehemiah said, "Go and enjoy choice food and sweet drinks, *and send some to those who have nothing prepared.* This day is holy to our Lord. Do not grieve, for the joy of the LORD is your strength" (Neh. 8:10 NIV; my italics). And later still, Jesus made the same point even more sharply in Luke 14:12–14.

Second, joy must be morally clean. In our fallen, sinful world, celebratory joy often descends into excesses of gluttony, drunkenness, and sexual promiscuity. As well as the warnings against such behavior in Israel's law, prophets, and wisdom literature, Israel also had two national object lessons when such behavior resulted in very severe divine judgment. One was at Mount Sinai itself, while Moses was receiving the Ten Commandments, when the people's wild orgy almost led to their complete destruction (Exod. 32–34). The other was at Baal Peor when they were tempted by the pagan seer Balaam into another orgy of sexual immorality (Num. 25; 31:16; and Deut. 4:3).

As Christians, some of us may need to be challenged to greater freedom in joyful celebration by the example of Jesus himself, who could enjoy a good party such as a wedding banquet (that usually went on for days) and is frequently recorded as eating and drinking with his friends (including those that nobody else would dream of eating with). "The Son of Man came eating and drinking," he said, when people contrasted him with the abstemious John the Baptist (Matt. 11:19). They criticized him for eating with tax collectors, prostitutes, and sinners. But clearly Jesus could enjoy food and drink without condoning sin and immorality.

Others of us may need to be challenged in the opposite direction, if we are tempted to allow our claim that we are simply exercising our Christian freedom and joy to descend into sinful excess.

The Bible does not forbid drinking wine, but it does forbid drunkenness (1 Cor. 5:11; Gal. 5:21; Eph. 5:18; 1 Pet. 4:3). It does not forbid enjoying our food, but it does condemn gluttony (Prov. 23:20–21; Tit. 1:12). It does not forbid humour and laughter, but it does forbid "obscenity, foolish talk or coarse joking" (Eph. 5:4) — the sort that is filthy or hurtful to others. The Bible gives us abundant room and reasons for joy, but warns us against letting celebration sink into degradation.[2]

I am sure Dan Denk will say amen to all of the above, and indeed these thoughts are expanded and given rich practical application in the chapters that follow. Enjoy!

Christopher J. H. Wright
Langham Partnership

2. Wright, *Cultivating the Fruit of the Spirit*, 45.

Introduction

Surprised by Joy — Again

I believe that we are made for joy, designed for joy, and I would say destined for joy. God's joy is in our blood.[1] We have both the capacity for joy and a deep yearning for joy. Even in this broken world, we can know true joy. At the same time, it often seems out of reach because so many foes are battling against it — worry, fear, doubt, grief, deceit, weariness, pervasive evil, and a deep sense of loss as we age. Our dreams begin to fade. All of these have the potential to rob us of our joy, and they often succeed. So many people in our culture live with deep regret rather than hope and contentment and joy.

The experience of joy is becoming rare. How many truly joyful people do you know? Do you consider yourself a joyful person? Would you like to have more joy in your life? Some people have given up on joy altogether and no longer expect to find it. They may have become disillusioned. They may feel that they have outgrown their need for joy. But for most of us, it is still the great prize we hope to find someday. We would love to know the secret of lasting joy.

But what is this joy we seek? Where do we find it? How can we nurture this elusive feeling, this state of mind? Is there a path to joy? These are all important questions that I plan to explore in the pages that follow.

Some of you are no doubt naturally more joyful than I am. I am skeptical by nature, blessed (and sometimes afflicted) with an analytical mind. I tend to focus on what's wrong with the world. I comfort myself with the notion that perhaps I am more of a prophet-type personality. I mean, the prophet Amos doesn't strike me as a particularly jolly person. True, I am not easily depressed or discouraged, but I am not easily *im*pressed either. And I am not easily pleased. When I have participated in gift-affirmation group exercises with friends and colleagues, their words for me are usually along the line of "steady," "unflappable," "level-headed," "balanced." Certainly not "lighthearted," "carefree," or "jovial."

This is why I was somewhat taken aback when on the occasion of my retirement from InterVarsity Christian Fellowship, a close friend and colleague of many years included in his note in my Appreciation Notebook, "You are a wise and deeply joyful man." How could he have gotten it so wrong? I thought he knew me well. At the same time, it got me thinking, more positively, that maybe I do have more joy in my life than I had realized.

Then there was the time when my oldest daughter was visiting — my missionary daughter, my Reformed charismatic daughter, my midwife daughter who delivers babies for fun. She is one of the gentlest people I know. As we sat around the breakfast table, just the two of us, she said, "Dad, you seem to have lost some of your joy lately." So, being the mature, understanding, approachable father that I am (after I got over my defensiveness and the dozen excuses that jumped into my mind), I said, "OK, tell me more." So she did. She also suggested a book to read: Mike Mason's *Champagne for the Soul: Rediscovering God's Gift of Joy*, whose ideas you will find scattered throughout these pages.

I have another daughter who is a naturally joyful person. When she was a child I called her my songbird. She was always singing, playful, and sunny-hearted. And still is. Indeed, her middle name is Joy, and it must have been prophetic. She loves a party, leads us in games, and lives a full life — very much an "in the moment" person. Recently, she got a small tattoo with the word "joy" in Tolkien's Elvish. Yet another daughter is marked by a childlike curiosity about life and, as a social worker, finds much joy in serving people, especially the disadvantaged. My son, a musician, told me he can hardly listen to Mozart's Requiem without being moved to tears. In many ways my children have been my teachers.

I have worked in campus ministry most of my life. I have encountered some students who seem to carry the weight of the world on their shoulders. Some come from broken families or are survivors of abuse. I worked with university students in the Balkans during the 1990s, and some of them were robbed of their childhood by the atrocities of war. They were cheated of that period of life that should have been filled with joy and wonder, innocence and play. A happy childhood is becoming an increasingly rare gift in our world.

For those of us who were blessed with a generally happy childhood, as we move into adulthood, we tend to leave our childlike joy behind, thinking of it as immature and naive. This is a big mistake and a tragic loss. We would do well to recapture that childlike joy with all its wonder and imagination and trust. And we can do it. More on that later.

Some of us, many of us, carry burdens that God never intended us to bear. We may have a messiah complex, thinking that it is up to us to solve the problems of the world, to fix people's hurts, to provide the answers. For those of us in the helping professions, this is a great temptation. Left unchecked, it can lead to resentment, disillusionment, and burnout.

Let me offer a preliminary definition of joy here so that we have a common idea of what we are talking about. Joy is definitely a feeling, though it is not simply that. Feelings tend to be fleeting. They are fickle. Joy, on the contrary, is *a steady disposition about life*, very much connected to peace and hope. We might say that joy is a hopeful and peaceful outlook on life, *a deep-seated sense of well-being*. Nor is joy the same as a pleasurable mood caused by the discharge of dopamine in the brain. Our desire for pleasure usually fails to bring us joy and may even steal our joy. Pleasure is individual; joy reaches beyond itself. Similar to love, joy is not self-serving but others-directed. Unlike happiness, joy is not dependent on circumstances. We can experience joy even in times of trouble and hardship. For example, we might say about someone, "Mary has been through a lot, yet she is a deeply joyful person."

Who wouldn't want to have more joy in their life? We humans have a natural yearning for it. But joy seems to be an elusive commodity. It often comes and goes as though it has a will of its own. Is there something we can do or need to do to experience more joy in our life? Why is it that some people seem to be more naturally joyful than others? If you have ever met a truly joyful person — and they are rare — you know they are very pleasing and fun to be around. You are naturally drawn to them, and you wonder — what is it that they have?

Joy as a By-Product

I have come to the conclusion that the reason joy is so elusive is because it is a by-product of something else. We are always joyful *over* something, something that we perceive as very good.[2] Joy is not the end itself. Joy will always have an object outside of ourselves — that thing or person in which we find our joy.[3] We don't find joy by straining to achieve it, and we don't find joy by solving some kind of riddle or puzzle or by following a formula. In short, we don't find joy by pursuing joy; we find it by pursuing something else. But if it is a *by*-product, a complement to something else, we might ask: What is the *product*? What is that other thing we need to know or have so that a deep sense of joy will flow over us? Keep reading. That is what I hope to make clear in the coming pages.

We can begin to get an answer to that "something else" by reflecting on the story of C. S. Lewis, who describes his own search for joy in his autobiography, *Surprised by Joy*. Lewis's mother died when he was eight years old. She was the life and light of their home. "With my mother's death all settled happiness, all that was tranquil and reliable, disappeared from my life" (21). His father rapidly fell into a deep depression. And so little Jack (nickname for Clive Staples) and his older brother, Warnie, felt as though they had lost both a mother and a father. They were soon sent away to boarding school. This turned out to be a horrendous experience for Jack especially. He continued to carry his sadness with him through school and private tutoring, then to Oxford University, interrupted by a stint in the army during World War I, then back to Oxford to finish his studies, and then as a lecturer at Oxford. By then, Lewis was a confirmed atheist. Yet he was searching for joy.

Along the way, his quest for joy led him to some literary friends, later known as the Inklings. Contemporary Christian intellectuals like J. R. R. Tolkien, Charles Williams, Hugo Dyson, and Owen Barfield were having an increasing influence on Lewis. "These queer people now seemed to pop up on every side" (216). He was also immersed in the writings of predecessors G. K. Chesterton, the great Christian apologist, and George MacDonald, the great Christian storyteller, whose writings had a continuing impact on

Lewis. In reading MacDonald's *Phantastes*, he records, "That night my imagination was, in a certain sense, baptized; the rest of me, not unnaturally, took longer" (181). MacDonald's fairy tales continued to cast their "bright shadow" of goodness upon Jack. "In reading Chesterton, as in reading MacDonald, I did not know what I was letting myself in for. A young man who wishes to remain a sound Atheist cannot be too careful of his reading" (191).

After numerous late-night conversations with his Oxford colleagues, some long walks, and much debate with his Inkling friends, especially Tolkien, Jack Lewis finally concluded that the Jesus story was the true story and, at age thirty-three, came to believe in a personal God and eventually in Jesus Christ as his Lord. He describes being "drug into the kingdom kicking, struggling, resentful, and darting his eyes in every direction for a chance of escape" (229). And yet the change in his life was extraordinary. Barfield described Lewis as "the most thoroughly converted man I have ever known."

He concludes this story of his early life with a question: And what of my quest for joy? To his surprise, he had lost interest in the quest. He realized that we don't find joy by chasing after it. Joy always comes as a surprise. It is a by-product of finding that great prize. Lewis had found joy beyond his wildest dreams in the most unexpected way: through his newfound faith in God and his commitment to Jesus. It was his quest for joy, almost like a divine carrot, that finally led him to the source of true joy. It was not to be found in the many philosophies and offerings of this world[4] but in that which transcends the natural world, in discovering the transcendent God as Creator and ultimately Jesus as Savior.

In *Mere Christianity*, Lewis puts it this way: "If I find in myself a desire which no experience in this world can satisfy, the most probable explanation is that I was made for another world."[5] And so, similarly, since we find a desire for joy in our deepest being, the explanation must be that we were made for joy. But it is a joy that we do not find in the promises and offerings of this world. It is found in that other world that transcends this one, another kingdom — a kingdom that has been inaugurated by Jesus himself and that awaits culmination.

But What About . . . ?

No doubt many of you, if you are like me, are beginning to feel uncomfortable and skeptical about this narrow focus on joy. You are possibly thinking, "Well yes, but what about when we are in physical and emotional pain? What about my friend who is chronically depressed, or who has lost a loved one?" I promise you that I do intend to deal with this objection in depth, and I am not proposing a Pollyanna view of life in which we are oblivious to suffering. If you feel you must first deal with this roadblock to move ahead, go to chapter 8, "Joy and Suffering."

Besides personal suffering, there's also suffering on a global scale. Rampant injustice, genocide, civil wars, millions of refugees and displaced people, children starving — the world is in such a mess. How can we be joyfully impervious to all the crying needs? Will we go about our merry way while the world goes to hell in a handbasket? Actually, joy does not close our eyes to the pressing needs around us. It is in fact the joy in our lives that gives us the strength and motivation to reach out to others in need. In George MacDonald's novel *Adela Cathcart*, he has Adela express it this way: "Take from me my joy and I am powerless to help others."[6]

Introduction

The Urgency of Christian Joy

I want to suggest a certain urgency about this message of Christian joy. First, for those of us who are followers of Jesus, we are promised joy. And each day that we live in gloomy despondency, in a dismal state of blah-ness, or in worry, fear, and anxiety, we are missing out on the full and abundant life Jesus intends for us. Jesus came into this world that we might have life in all its fullness (John 10:10). To his disciples he said, "These things I have spoken to you, that my joy may be in you, and that your joy may be full" (John 15:11). Jesus looked at the multitudes with compassion and amazement that they could mistake their drab existence for real *life* — "harassed and helpless, like sheep without a shepherd" (Matt. 9:36). We were made for joyous fullness of life. We are destined for joy, finally leading into eternity.

Second, it is also urgent that we claim this joy because the world desperately needs to see it in the lives of Christians and in the Christian community. The world is a dark place, and Jesus came to bring light. As Alexander Schmemann says, "Jesus died for the life of the world."[7] Our world is full of weary, weighed-down people who need to see what a life of joy looks like. Current studies seem to point to unprecedented rates of suicide, depression, self-injury, anxiety, loneliness, and detachment in today's young people. Millennials and Gen Zs (born 1995 or later) are not known as particularly jubilant people. In fact, the emerging generation is sometimes labeled the "ticked off" generation. They are not happy with the hand they have been dealt. They need to be invited into the life of joy and fullness that Jesus offers.

More than ever, the best apologetic for Christian truth that we can present to the watching world is a community of love and joy and peace; a Christian community of people who know how to live life wholeheartedly, purposefully, and generously. We need to be the church, caught up in joyful worship and giving of ourselves in joyful service — "that they may see [our] good works and give glory to [our] Father who is in heaven" (Matt. 5:14–16). Our calling is to offer a model of a life of joy, even in persecution, hardship, and suffering (Matt. 5:11–12; James 1:2).

Finally, this message is urgent because of some worrying developments in our society. Charles Mathewes, professor of religious studies at the University of Virginia, contends that in our modern technological culture, people seem to be increasingly losing their capacity for real joy.[8] In terms of material comforts, we have never had it so good. We can also applaud the achievements of medical science. But along with these advancements has emerged an endless number of nonstop diversions now at our fingertips (smartphones and other such devices), which provide a massive escapism so that we need never consider the truly important questions of life. These evasions are "a way of staving off the contemplation of the emptiness of our lives."[9] When and how will people pause to even ask the basic question "What is it that makes life worth living?"

Our deepest longings and best desires are being drowned out by the noise, the clutter, and the distractions that are so readily available to us. And with this, our capacity for joy is withering. Many today express their concern for a generation that finds it difficult to focus or to maintain a train of thought for an extended length of time. But I worry that we may be witnessing a generation with a diminished ability to live fully, to live abundantly, and to enter wholly into the joy that makes life truly worth living.

Miroslav Volf, professor of theology at Yale Divinity School, has been leading a project called God and Human Flourishing for several years, inviting scholars to present papers on joy, the good life, life worth living. This is a noble effort and one that strikes at the heart of the most important questions of life, questions that often get lost in the highly technocratic university curriculum with its shrinking interest in the humanities. We will be seeing more on this project in the pages that follow.

The Blueprint for This Book

Here are the questions I have been pondering: What is the Christian understanding of joy? Was Jesus a joyful person? Are Christians supposed to be joyful? What if we lose our joy? How can we restore it?

As I worked through this study of joy, and as I have walked the journey of joy for several years now, I began to realize that joy can be a lens through which to view and understand the whole life of the Christian. It has become for me a window into what it means to be a Christian, living in awe of God's gracious gifts of creation, God's saving work in the world, and the joyful destiny God has determined for us. It is also a means to understand the place of the church in the world.

Bookstores are already filled with self-help books about how to find happiness, and this is not going to be one of them. But still we may ask: Where might we find this great prize called joy? Is there a road to joy? What is conducive to joy, and what detracts from it? How might we cultivate joy in our lives?

In chapter 1 we will consider the invitation to joy that emerges from the created world in which we live, as well as from the poetry of the Hebrew Bible and from the entry of Jesus into this world. In chapter 2 I offer an extended definition of joy. Chapter 3 takes a closer look at Jesus. Was Jesus a joyful person? What did he mean when he said, "My joy I give to you"? In chapter 4 we pursue the question "Where is this joy to be found?" We will find answers in some of the parables of Jesus, which reveal a surprising correlation between "finding joy" and "being found." This is where I will share more of my own journey, and we will find illustrations from Tolkien and Bunyan. Chapter 5 is an invitation to remember and revisit our childlike joy. Chapters 6 and 7 will look at "friends of joy" and "enemies of joy." They may not be what you expect. In chapter 8 we finally delve into the issue of joy and suffering. These two ideas regularly appear side by side in the Bible. Is it possible to have joy even in suffering? We will learn from Joni Eareckson Tada and other experts. Drawing on Mother Teresa and others, chapter 9 deals with joy in service. And chapter 10 explores joy in worship, especially as expressed in the Psalms. Chapter 11 is "Joy to the World," where we'll consider how desperately this world needs the experience of joy. Such joy, such fullness of life, is offered to every person. Lastly, in chapter 12 I propose that we are destined for joy. This explains the longing in our hearts for the "happy ending" often demonstrated in Hollywood films. It explains our yearning for a world of love, a world without sighing and crying and dying, a world of uninterrupted bliss!

I certainly do not claim to have mastered the experience of joy, but on this journey, I have been learning some important and surprising clues to finding greater joy.

I invite you to come along and walk with me for a while on this road to joy.

Reflection Questions

1. Think of a time in your life when you were especially happy, very joyful. What were the circumstances?
2. Would you say that this is a particularly joyful time in your life right now? How would you rate your joy meter on a scale of 1–10?

3. Do you think that God wants you to be joyful? What is the basis for this belief?

4. We will explore this more later, but if you are not feeling very joyful these days, what would you say is the primary thing that robs your joy?

5. Do you know someone who truly exudes joy? What is it about them, do you think, that is the secret to their joy? It's okay if you have no idea.

I

God Invites Us to Joy

Frederick Buechner tells the story of a road trip from New York to Pennsylvania for a speaking engagement. He was determined to stay in the present and to focus on what he was seeing. After a while he started noticing the trees:

> They were in full summer foliage. They were greener than I could remember ever having seen trees before. The sun was in them. The air was stirring them. As I drove by, they waved their leafy branches at me like plumes. They beckoned. They reached out. . . . They waved in the only way trees have of waving and caught my attention so completely that other thoughts vanished from my head, including my thoughts about them. I didn't think about them. I just saw them. I didn't put words to what was happening. I just let it happen. . . .
>
> The trees are always so glad to see us. That was the best way I could find to say it. They waved their branches like flags in a parade, hailing me as I passed by as though I was some mighty spirit. They looked as if they had lined up for miles along the New York Thruway to greet me, and after a while I started waving back at them from time to time as if they too were mighty spirits and it was I who was greeting them.[1]

As I have said, I am on a journey of joy. On this journey I have searched carefully through the biblical accounts to try to understand what they have to say about joy. And I have been surprised, pleasantly surprised, to find that the Scriptures have a great deal to say about our yearning for joy and the expression of joy in our lives, as well as what it is and where to find it.

The Old Testament is bursting with joy. Biblical Hebrew has several terms for "joy" and thirteen roots for words that express the exuberance of life of the people of God in response to God's greatness and goodness toward them.[2] These Hebrew words, as expressions of joy, are often translated into English as "merriment," "gladness," "happy," "laughter," "wonder," "exuberance," "exulting," "praise," "worship," "shout," "sing," "delight," and "blessed."

Even "dancing" becomes a legitimate expression for joy, as in "you have turned for me my mourning into dancing, you removed my sackcloth and clothed me with joy" (Ps. 30:11).[3]

The Natural World Invites Us to Joy

The poetry of the Hebrew Bible represents the whole of creation as already caught up in the dance of joy and wonder of the Creator. The earth is full of praising and rejoicing. When the world was first made, we are told that "the morning stars sang together, and all the sons of God shouted for joy" (Job 38:7). The mountains and the hills continue to burst forth with joy. The water in the brook is bubbling with laughter. The trees of the forest are clapping their hands. It is all a marvelous invitation for us to join the created world in this procession of gladness and praise. It is as though the whole creation is saying, "What are you waiting for? Don't you get it? You people of faith, you children of God, surely you would want to join in the dance as well!"

The psalmist repeats the same joyful picture over and over again:

> The pastures of the wilderness overflow,
>> the hills gird themselves with joy,
> the meadows clothe themselves with flocks,
>> the valleys deck themselves with grain,
>> they shout and sing together for joy. (Ps. 65:12–13)

> Let the heavens be glad, and let the earth rejoice;
>> let the sea roar, and all that fills it;
>> let the field exult, and everything in it!
> Then shall all the trees of the forest sing for joy
>> before the LORD, for he comes,
>> for he comes to judge the earth. (Ps. 96:11–13a)

> Let the rivers clap their hands;
>> let the hills sing for joy together
> before the LORD, for he comes
>> to judge the earth. (Ps. 98:8–9a)

In Genesis 1 we are left with the inescapable conclusion that the Creator God takes joy in his creative work. He steps back and considers all that he has made and declares that it is "very good" (Gen. 1:31). Now the whole creation is pictured as rejoicing in God's goodness (Isa. 44:23; 49:13). God's creative work, and his continued care of his creation, is such that the world is full of abundance and color and design and liveliness. Because of this, the Hebrew poets could personify even the inanimate world as singing and dancing and clapping and shouting with joy.

No wonder Buechner, in his story, began to feel that the trees were waving to him. Have you ever waved back at the trees? Have you ever been moved to shout for joy, to clap your hands, or to sing of the wonders of God's beauty? I remember driving down the highway in Northern Michigan one autumn. The oranges and golds of the leaves were so lush, striking, and bountiful that I found myself praising God out loud, with tears streaming down my face. I was moved, as in the Keith Green song, to say, "O Lord, you're beautiful, your face is all I see." I have a neighbor who has a glorious display of rose vines. From time to time she puts up a sign for passersby that says, "Stop and smell the roses." I do. Indeed, we would all do well to take time to smell the roses, to notice the many shades of color, and to rejoice in their intricate shapes.

Come to the Feast

Through his prophet Isaiah, God gives a generous and happy invitation:

> "Come, everyone who thirsts,
> come to the waters;
> and he who has no money,
> come, buy and eat!
> Come, buy wine and milk
> without money and without price.
> Why do you spend your money for that which
> is not bread,
> and your labor for that which does not satisfy?
> Listen diligently to me, and eat what is good,
> and delight yourselves in rich food.
> Incline your ear, and come to me;
> hear, that your soul may live." (Isa. 55:1–3)

This is the most generous, mind-boggling invitation you will find anywhere in any sacred writings, one that Jesus extends with his own rendering in Matthew 11:28, as we will see later in the chapter. The picture presented is one of a great banquet prepared with all manner of food and drink. All you have to do is *come*. The invitation to "come" is repeated three times in the original passage (followed by three calls to *listen*, conveying urgency). It is a free and open invitation to any who will come in faith and partake. Note the irony of coming and "buying," but without money. It is true that there is a price to be paid, but it is not the guests' to pay. Their part is simply to repent and receive. As the passage moves on, it becomes clear that what is being offered is not merely food and drink but the Lord himself, along with his mercy, love, and pardon — "that your soul may live." "Seek the LORD while he may be found; call upon him while he is near" (Isa. 55:6).[4]

At the conclusion of this passage, Isaiah makes a breathtaking promise:

> "For you shall go out in joy
>   and be led forth in peace;
> the mountains and the hills before you
>   shall break forth into singing,
>   and all the trees of the field shall clap their hands.
> Instead of the thorn shall come up the cypress;
>   instead of the brier shall come up the myrtle;
> and it shall make a name for the LORD,
>   an everlasting sign that shall not be cut off."
>
> (Isa. 55:12–13)

You shall "go out" (harkening back to Exodus) from your captivity — only the liberation Isaiah has in mind is more than just physi-

cal; it is liberation that involves complete spiritual transformation,
one in which the creation itself is released from its bondage into a
newfound joy. The curse and its effects, the "thorn" and the "brier,"
are also removed as paradise is restored (cf. Rom. 8:18–21).[5]

As with Israel of old, so it is today. Do we still have eyes to see
and ears to hear? Has our imagination and sense of expectation
grown dull? Have we become so removed from the natural world
that we have lost sight of the wonder and the beauty that are there?
Can we no longer hear the song of the ages and creation's invitation
for us to join in the celebration? Can we still hear the voice of God
with his promises of a better world that is already breaking into
this old world of ours? And can we accept his invitation to come
and find that which truly satisfies, so that our souls may live? This
is his invitation to joy, to the flourishing life.

The Lord Rejoices over Us?

The prophet Zephaniah speaks of the restoration of God's people
with this joy-filled promise:

> Sing aloud, O daughter of Zion;
>> shout, O Israel!
> *Rejoice* and *exult* with all your heart,
>> O daughter of Jerusalem!
> The LORD has taken away the judgments against you;
>> he has cleared away your enemies.
> The King of Israel, the LORD, is in your midst;
>> you shall never again fear evil.
> On that day it shall be said to Jerusalem:
>> "Fear not, O Zion;
>> let not your hands grow weak.

The LORD your God is in your midst,
    a mighty one who will save;
he will *rejoice* over you with *gladness*;
    he will quiet you by his love;
he will *exult* over you with loud singing."

(Zeph. 3:14–17, emphasis mine)

Again, the prophet calls the people to an appropriately joyful response to God's goodness and mercy toward them. But in verse 17, the view changes by saying that it is *God* who will rejoice and exult with gladness — over *you!* The first time I read this line, I was puzzled. I thought it must be a mistranslation. Really? God will delight in his people? He looks on me with a big, perhaps tearful, smile, with joy and loud singing? That is an overwhelming image to take in. But that is the truth, brothers and sisters; that is the truth.

And this is not the only place we find this bold statement. Isaiah paints the same picture in his description of the restoration: "As the bridegroom rejoices over the bride, so shall your God rejoice over you" (Isa. 62:5). Have you seen the look on the face of the groom at a wedding when he sees his bride walking down the aisle? He is beaming with a joy that is almost impossible to contain. That is the picture of God rejoicing over us.

A similar image that comes to my mind is one from the final scenes in the *Lord of the Rings* trilogy. At the end of the film version, the four hobbits are finally reunited after a long, arduous, wayward journey. They are jumping up and down on the bed where Frodo is just waking up. Then Gandalf enters the room and looks on them with great joy. He smiles, then begins to chuckle, then lets out a full belly laugh, tears streaming down his cheeks. This scene reminds me of how God himself rejoices over us after we have come through hard-fought battles.

Why is it so hard for us to live in the picture the prophets offer us? Is it because we feel unworthy? Perhaps we have become so accustomed to the idea of God frowning on us over our failures and futile efforts to please him. We find it hard to believe that, in his forgiveness, he would actually smile on us and delight in us. But that is how radical God's grace really is toward us.

I am reminded of Eric Liddell's famous rejoinder in *Chariots of Fire*. When his sister tries to convince him to give up running in the Olympics and come serve Christ in China, he promises that he will go to China, but for now "God made me fast, and when I run, I feel his pleasure." Do we feel God's pleasure? Ever?

I served as a camp director at InterVarsity's Cedar Campus for five years. During that time I joined our faithful crew in cleaning up after our guests. As we moved from room to room and cabin to cabin, we were aware that no one would likely notice the extra loving care we gave to our task or the effort we put into the most demanding cleanup jobs. But I had a persistent sense that God's smile was upon us, because he notices even "what we do in secret" (Matt. 6:4). And I sensed his pleasure. When we grasp this truth, even the humblest act of service is transformed into something sacred and is a cause for joy.

Consider also the doxology/benediction in Jude 24: "Now to him who is able to keep you from stumbling and to present you blameless before the presence of his glory with great joy . . ." The thought of one day being presented before God's throne, without fault or blemish because of our union with the One who was fully without blemish, is surely beyond what we can comprehend. It is indeed cause for great rejoicing — on our part, for the angels, and even for God himself.[6]

And this promise is not only for the future restoration. The Scriptures assure us that whenever we offer sincere worship to God, whenever we give generously to the Lord's work, whenever we offer acts of service as to the Lord — our loving, heavenly Father sees our deeds and is well pleased. We can be sure that his smile is upon us (Heb. 13:16; Phil. 3:18; Col. 3:23–24; Mic. 6:7–8; Matt. 6:3–4).

Jean Sophia Pigott captures this truth in her tender hymn "Jesus I Am Resting, Resting" from 1876, which contains the line "Resting 'neath thy smile, Lord Jesus . . ." When I first sang this verse many years ago, I was a bit shy about making such a claim — that Jesus smiles on me — but it has since grown on me, and now I love to dwell on that great thought.

Why am I spending so much time on this point? Because I believe we are missing out on many joyful moments, and we are missing the full scope of God's gracious invitation to us. When it begins to sink in that God, the Almighty God, the Great King, because of his great love and mercy, *rejoices over us*, our hearts cannot help but well up with joy.

Jesus Comes with Joy

In the New Testament, Jesus's physical presence on earth is bookended by expressions of joy. With his arrival we have the familiar message of the angels to the shepherds: "Do not be afraid. I bring you good news that will cause great joy for all the people" (Luke 2:10). We are also told that the wise men "rejoiced with exceeding great joy" when they saw the guiding star (Matt. 2:10). Even before that, the announcements of Jesus's coming are accompanied by joy. Gabriel tells Zechariah that he and Elizabeth "will have joy and gladness" on account of their son John, the forerunner to Christ, "and many will rejoice at his birth" (Luke 1:14), and in Mary's Magnificat she declares, "My soul magnifies the Lord, and my spirit rejoices in God my Savior" (Luke 1:46). The coming of

Jesus into this world is a joyful occasion, and the central characters are caught up in the celebration.

The same is true of his departure. The resurrection of Jesus brings joy to the hearts of his disciples. It was almost more than they could have hoped for. They couldn't believe their eyes. "And while they still disbelieved for joy and were marveling, he said to them, 'Have you anything here to eat?'" (Luke 24:41). Jesus had to eat some food with them in order for it to really sink in. After Jesus's resurrection and ascension, the final words of Luke's Gospel tell how the disciples "worshiped him and returned to Jerusalem with great joy, and were continually in the temple blessing God" (Luke 24:52–53).

"The New Testament is the most buoyant, exhilarating, and joyful book in the world," says the Scottish theologian James Denney.[7] Christianity is a religion of joy.[8] "Joy is the rubric over all of Christendom."[9] The coming of Jesus the Messiah brings great joy. People are brought to a new outlook or attitude toward life, as were the twelve apostles, the women who followed Jesus, and the multitudes who were fed, healed, delivered, and touched by Jesus's teaching and the offer of the kingdom of heaven.

Jesus Invites Us into His Joyful Kingdom

During Jesus's earthly ministry, he continually proclaimed, "Repent, for the kingdom of heaven is at hand" (Matt. 3:2; 4:17). The invitation to enter this new kind of kingdom goes hand in hand with the invitation to joy. This joy is received by means of entering the kingdom. It is a result, an outcome. When we respond to Jesus's generous offer of the kingdom, and to Jesus as King, we find joy unspeakable. Jesus summed it up this way: "seek first the kingdom of God and his righteousness, and all these things will be added to you" (Matt. 6:33). The promise of *all these things* refers back to "what you eat," "what you drink," "what you wear," but it also includes the wonderful gift of *joy*, which comes by rising above worry and fear (see chapter 7).

This is why I have said that we don't find joy by seeking joy; we find joy by seeking the kingdom. We find it by living well — that is, by living life the way God intended for us. Joy is a by-product of God's inbreaking kingdom. And receiving the kingdom comes by receiving the rule of King Jesus in our lives.

Hear the words of Jesus:

> "Come to me, all who labor and are heavy laden, and I will give you rest. Take my yoke upon you, and learn from me, for I am gentle and lowly in heart, and you will find rest for your souls. For my yoke is easy, and my burden is light." (Matt. 11:28–30)

We find joy by simply resting in the arms of Jesus. When we come to him, abandoning all our striving, casting aside our self-help formulas and our attempts to go it alone, and instead casting ourselves at his feet — we find joy. Come, all you who are thirsty for something more than your weary life is giving you. Come, all you who are caught in this dreary, humdrum existence that you mistake for *life*. I am offering you something that money cannot buy. Why settle for that which does not satisfy, when God is offering us true bread and spiritual food beyond our wildest imagination — life in all its fullness.

Notice that Jesus's invitation is not "come to my new set of teachings" or "come to my new religion"; it is "come to *me*, and I will give you rest." It is a daring claim, and one that can be made only by the Son of God.

We also find joy, ironically, by coming under Jesus's yoke. A yoke is a wooden bar attached to an ox or pair of oxen to guide them in the proper direction for plowing a field. But Jesus's yoke is "easy" and "light." He is not a harsh taskmaster. He is the one who made us and loves us and knows us completely. He knows how we are made and why we were made. His yoke is designed to fit us perfectly, not to take away our freedom or creativity. His yoke is where we belong, where we are the most free, where we can rest in his love, and where we find unfathomable joy.

The Beatitudes, or "blessed are" statements, of Matthew 5:1–12 are an invitation to enter the joy of the kingdom. Blessedness is another synonym for joy. And the first beatitude is the key to them all: "Blessed are the poor in spirit, for theirs is the kingdom of heaven." Those who recognize their spiritual poverty truly understand the topsy-turvy nature of the kingdom Jesus is describing and what a great prize he is offering them. It is our pride that keeps us from the lighthearted humility that leads to joy. It keeps us from understanding and receiving the salvation Jesus offers. It is pride, more than anything else, that keeps people from embracing Jesus as their own Savior and King. In the *Divine Comedy*, Dante describes his imagined experience climbing Mount Purgatory. His task is wearisome, but when an angel's wing brushes off one of the *p*'s (for pride) from his forehead, his climb is much less arduous. Once we have dealt with our pride problem, the going is a lot less burdensome and more joyful. We will come back to this in chapter 3.

Could We Be Allergic to Joy?

Maybe we have difficulty imagining that God takes that much interest in us, or that he notices even the small things we do for his glory — speaking a grateful or encouraging word to a nurse, helping an international student buy a car, providing a meal for a family.

Yet Jesus promised that "your father who sees in secret will reward you" (Matt. 6:4).

Why is that so difficult to grasp? Why don't we live into this truth more often and find the joy that is waiting for us? It almost seems as if we are allergic to joy at times. Maybe we are afraid of too much joy, or we feel undeserving.

On the radio show *This American Life*, Chris Higgins tells the story "I've Fallen in Love and I Can't Get Up." It is the true story of Matt Frerking, who suffers from narcolepsy (falling asleep involuntarily during waking hours) and cataplexy.[10] This story was later developed into a film.[11] As it turns out, 70 percent of people who have narcolepsy also have cataplexy — the uncontrollable muscle weakness and temporary paralysis brought about by intense emotional feelings, especially laughter and feelings of happiness. In Matt's case, whenever he would begin to have feelings of love, his whole body would immediately collapse, and he would seem catatonic. As you can imagine, this condition put a serious damper on his romantic life, and he has had to develop some significant workarounds in order to enjoy many of life's happy moments.

Although we may not be encumbered with cataplexy, could it be that we also have an unfavorable reaction to the feeling of joy? Does it sometimes seem as though we are allergic to too much joy? As we have seen, everywhere God and his creation are inviting us to enter into joyful celebration. But maybe we feel we don't deserve that much happiness. Maybe we don't trust people who are overexuberant. Maybe we don't trust the joy, worried that it will soon fade away. We may be reacting against demonstrations of false joy. Perhaps we have met people who are incorrigibly optimistic, oblivious to the suffering around them and maybe even in denial about evil and pain. We have all encountered people who see the world through rose-colored glasses, as getting better and better every day. It may be the toxic positivity syndrome, which refuses to harbor or consider a negative thought.

I get that, and I struggle with the same issues. But we all need to rethink our inhibitions about joy so that we don't miss out on what God intends for us, and so that the world doesn't miss out on seeing this joy in action and thus witnessing precious evidence of God's invitation to them as well.

Let's not send this incredible invitation back to God unopened.

Reflection Questions

1. The Old Testament poetry portrays the whole of creation, the natural world, bursting with joy. How do you respond to this? Can you relate to this?

2. Do you experience joy when you encounter the beauty and aliveness of the creation? How often do you get out into "nature"?

3. Scripture also states that God takes joy in us, his people. Do you often sense God's pleasure, God's smile upon you? Why or why not?

4. Jesus invites us into his joyful kingdom. Have you responded to this invitation? Have you begun to find joy and rest and peace in being a member of his kingdom?

5. Do you sometimes wonder whether you are "allergic" to joy? Have you given up on joy? Do you wonder whether you have some kind of deficiency that prevents you from experiencing joy? Read on!

2

What Is This Joy We Seek?

In the 2006 movie *The Pursuit of Happyness* (their spelling), starring Will Smith and his son in real life, Jaden, we find Smith as a single parent, out of work, evicted from his apartment, sleeping in homeless shelters, standing in food lines with his son, and desperately trying to find a way out. It is a heartwarming story, based loosely on Smith's own rags-to-riches life experience. At one point, Smith's character, Chris Gardner, reflects:

> It was right then that I started thinking about Thomas Jefferson on the Declaration of Independence and the part about our right to life, liberty, and the pursuit of happiness. And I remember thinking, How did he know to put the "pursuit" part in there? That maybe happiness is something that we can only pursue and maybe we can actually never have it. No matter what. How did he know that?

Chris Gardner finally gets a break and becomes a highly successful, multimillionaire stockbroker. As one reviewer, Paul Arendt, comments: "The film deserves kudos for avoiding saccharine sentiment, but its relentless emphasis on money as the cure for all ills is depressing."¹ Indeed, this is the disappointing message of the film, in effect perpetuating the notion that wealth is the key to happiness. The pursuit of happiness is viewed as an inalienable right in the American Declaration of Independence, which in our day seems to be equated with the private pursuit of material goods.² So, what is this joy we seek? Is it the same as happiness? How is it related to pleasure?

Joy as a Hopeful, Peaceful Outlook on Life

In one sense, joy is not really that hard to understand. We don't need to demystify joy. We all know it when we see it, or when we feel it. However, I am finding that joy is not quite so easy to define or describe. Let me offer this preliminary definition of joy: *a deep-seated sense of well-being, often expressed by mirth.*

It is certainly true that joy, in one sense, is an emotion; it is something we feel. But joy is not simply a feeling or an emotion. Emotions can be momentary and passing. Joy is deeper, sturdier, weightier. It is not oblivious to circumstances but is resilient, often in spite of circumstances. It is a steady *disposition* and a hopeful, peaceful *outlook* on life. Joy accompanies a spirit of contentment. It is a state of mind.

We would expect joy to be expressed in some sort of merriment, though with our varying personalities, that will look different. Not everyone has a bubbly temperament. But if someone says, "I am really a joyful person," and there is no evidence that they are joyful, then we have reason to be skeptical. If a person has a persistently sour disposition, we would rightly question their claim to joy. Joy is invariably connected to laughter; it might be a belly laugh, a chuckle, or even tears of laughter. In *The Screwtape Letters*,

C. S. Lewis talks about four kinds of laughter or humor: joy, fun, the joke proper, and flippancy.[3] The highest and most sublime by far is the laughter that emerges naturally from joy. Screwtape has no idea where this kind of laughter comes from and views it as a grave danger to the devil's cause. Whereas flippancy, or cynicism, in which the joke is always assumed to already have been told, is the most useful for the schemes of the Evil One. What is expressed in this case is more of a scoff than a laugh.

Joy and Pleasure

At the same time, joy is not just a self-directed attitude; it is always others-directed and is lived out in community. Christian joy will always lead us into life with others. Some in our individualistic culture, or who practice Eastern religions, may speak of the inward gaze, a placid kind of joy and peace that is untroubled by the sadness of others. But true joy emerges from a generous, magnanimous spirit, understanding that God's grace is limitless and bountiful. Paul reminds us to "rejoice with those who rejoice, weep with those who weep" (Rom. 12:15).

Joy is not merely a pleasurable feeling brought on by a chemical reaction in the brain. In popular culture, dopamine is viewed as the brain's pleasure chemical, which can be produced by addictive drugs, sex, eating, or the anticipation of reward. The dependence on this chemical leads to the desire for greater and greater levels of arousal. In any case, joy is quite distinct from pleasure, and sometimes they are at opposite poles, since the pursuit of pleasure can at times rob us of our joy.

The psalmist contrasts real joy with the pleasurable feeling that is brought on by a bountiful harvest and an abundance of wine:

There are many who say, "Who will show us some
good?
Lift up the light of your face upon us, O LORD!"
You have put more joy in my heart
than they have when their grain and wine abound.
In peace I will both lie down and sleep;
for you alone, O LORD, make me dwell in safety.

(Ps. 4:6–8)

David speaks of a joy that is deeper and more satisfying than even
the pleasure of an abundant harvest, with full barns and bursting
wine cellars. John Calvin represents those whose "grain and wine
abound" as "being so bent upon, addicted to the pursuit of worldly
prosperity, as to have no thought of God, . . . but their joy in the
abundance and increase of their wine and corn is not so great as his
[David's] joy in the sense of the divine goodness alone."[4] Worldly
pleasure will never provide peaceful sleep and the solid joy that
comes from knowing God's favor shining upon us.

Joy is at the center of who we are as human beings in relationship with God. The Westminster Catechism asks, "What is the
chief end of man? Answer: To glorify God and enjoy him forever."
Enjoying God is not some add-on or frill. It is not a secondary experience intended for only a few saints. It is central to what it means
to be human, God's creation. It is God's deepest desire for us.

Joy versus Happiness

We often use "joy" and "happiness" as synonyms, but they are not
identical. Happiness tends to be somewhat fickle, dependent on the
changing circumstances of life. In his book *The Second Mountain*, David Brooks offers a helpful contrast between joy and happiness.

Happiness is great. But we only get one life, so we might as well use it for hunting for big game; to enjoy happiness, but to surpass happiness toward joy. Happiness tends to be individual; we measure it by asking, "Are you happy?" Joy tends to be self-transcending. Happiness is something you pursue; joy is something that rises up unexpectedly and sweeps over you. Happiness comes from accomplishments; joy comes from offering gifts. Happiness fades; we get used to the things that used to make us happy. Joy doesn't fade. To live with joy is to live with wonder, gratitude, and hope.[5]

I have a friend who says, "Happiness depends on the happenings." We sometimes use the word "happiness" with reference to our being in a good mood or having good fortune. The root word "hap" suggests good luck, closely related to happenstance or chance.

Even in common usage in our culture, most people seem to recognize a distinction between joy and happiness. In her sociological research, Brené Brown says people consistently described happiness as "an emotion that is connected to circumstances, and they described joy as a spiritual way of engaging with the world that is connected to the practice of gratitude."[6] This is an important insight and links joy to the idea of being "blessed." We will look at this below in connection with Jesus's teaching of the Beatitudes.

Joy is something deeper, fuller, more durable than happiness, like being fully alive. It looks back to God's goodness in our lives and reaches forward to a certain future. C. S. Lewis says joy must have "the stab, the pang, the inconsolable longing."[7]

Joy in Action

We might benefit by comparing joy and love. Most people would probably agree that *love* is more than a feeling; it is also an action

31

and a decision. A colleague of mine once confided in me that he no longer had any feelings of love for his wife. After some further discussion and reflection, I said, "Why don't you just start acting loving toward her, do loving acts, and see if your feelings change." A few months later he told me it was working; he had genuine loving feelings for his wife again. C. S. Lewis makes this point: "When you are behaving as if you loved someone, you will presently come to love them."[8] The same is true with hatred. For example, the Nazis no doubt hated the Jews, but when they treated the Jews with brutality, they despised them all the more.[9] When we treat others inhumanely, it follows that we will begin to view them as less than human. Feelings follow behavior.

So it is with joy. It often comes to us by taking some positive action, by changing our outlook, by making a decision toward joy. Mike Mason concludes, "Joy is like a muscle, and the more you exercise it, the stronger it grows."[10] The more we live into joy, the more natural it becomes. Kay Warren, in her book *Joy Is a Choice You Can Make Today*, makes helpful observations along this line, that joy is a daily choice.[11] Otherwise, the command to "rejoice" would be meaningless.

Maybe you've had the experience of feeling rather gloomy, then you become aware of it and think, "Now why am I feeling this way?" There may be no obvious reason we are feeling gloomy. It may have been some trivial thing — the store was closed, the appointment got changed, someone cut me off in traffic, I have indigestion. When we bring it out into the light and look at it, we can often change our outlook very quickly and positively back toward joy.

But this is not the whole of the matter either. It is not simply an act of the will. We don't just *will* joy into being. It is a response to some greater truth, some deeper reality. If it is honest and sincere joy, it must have some basis, some reason connected to reality. It is time to take a careful look at the New Testament teachings about joy.

Joy in the New Testament

The various Greek words for "joy" occur 326 times in the New Testament. Whenever we embark on a thematic study in the Bible, we must of course consider all the numerous occurrences and variations of the word in its various contexts. But we also need to consider other passages where the idea of joy is described but using different words. A concordance study is helpful but by itself can be limiting. It is only the beginning.

The most common New Testament word for "joy" is *chara* in Greek (146 times), and it is typically translated "joy," "joyful," "delight," and "gladness." In its verb form, we see it often as a command: *Rejoice!* It is closely related to the word "grace," *charis*. Clearly, it is God's grace, in our lives and in the world, that is the occasion for joy. God's gracious work in creation and redemption — the beauty of creation, the forgiveness of sins, the resurrection of Jesus, the new abundant life we are offered in Christ, and the promise of our own resurrection — these are all grounds for Christian joy. Wonder, gratitude, and hope are good gifts of a good God that bring us joy. This points us to another related word, *charismata*, which carries the idea of "gift." Joy is the human response to the goodness of God in his manifold gifts. And I would also say it is God's "common grace" that is able to bring about joy in the hearts of all people, even those who do not acknowledge God's gracious gifts.

I have already noted that joy is closely related to the word "blessed." If we ask, Who are the truly joyful people?, then we must turn to Jesus and the Beatitudes (Matt. 5:3–12). In these eight "blessed are" declarations, Jesus was basically saying, "Let me tell you who the really lucky people are. These are the people to be congratulated, because they have found what is truly important and satisfying in life. And it is not who you might think. These are the people I declare to be the *blessed* ones — the poor in spirit, the meek, those who mourn, those who hunger and thirst for righteousness, the merciful, the pure in heart, the peacemakers, the persecuted." In saying this, Jesus surely turned conventional wisdom on its head, replacing it with new kingdom values of pure joy.

If we watch TV ads for just ten minutes and make a list of who the blessed people are according to the ads, our list might look more like this: Blessed are the wealthy, the famous, the beautiful, the young, the healthy, the athletic, the people with the most toys, those with the most exciting experiences, the best food, the best drink, the best cars, and the best insurance policies. These ads make grand promises, but do they really deliver? The products or services they sell may give you a rush of excitement, a passing feeling of importance, but they will not provide an enduring joy. No, when we look at Jesus's description of the "blessed" people, we see that the qualities they have are not for sale; they are not commodities to be consumed. I wonder what a Super Bowl ad (costing five million dollars for thirty seconds) would look like if it was promoting the value of being "poor in spirit" or "merciful." I think we sense, deep down inside, that these kingdom qualities of Jesus are in fact the real path of joy, that for which our hearts truly long.

Joy as the Fruit of the Spirit

As we seek to understand the nature of joy, it is important to remember that joy is a fruit of the Spirit, and as such it is the work of God's Spirit in us:

But the fruit of the Spirit is love, joy, peace, patience, kindness,
goodness, faithfulness, gentleness, self-control; against such
things there is no law. (Gal. 5:22–23)

With this in view, we see that joy is a gift of God. This joy is God-
ward in its focus and others-directed, not turned in on one's self.
Joy is the result of the quality of our relationship with God and a
concern for the well-being of others.

The fruit of the Spirit stands in contrast to the works of sinful
flesh — sexual immorality, impurity, and debauchery; idolatry and
witchcraft; hatred, discord, jealousy, fits of rage, selfish ambition,
dissensions, factions and envy; drunkenness, orgies, and the like
(Gal. 5:19–21). Look at this list. One thing is clear: these things do
not bring joy. They are self-indulgent rather than God-focused,
and they put the self before others. Imagine being caught up in the
prison of jealousy or in a fit of rage and trying to be joyful at the
same time. It will never happen. Even sexual pleasure, apart from
God's design for sex in a committed marriage relationship, will not
provide the deep satisfaction and connection we seek.

Joy in Relation to Love and Peace

It is important to notice that the "joy" fruit, in Paul's fruit of the
Spirit passage, is sandwiched between "love" and "peace." This
gives us more understanding of the nature of genuine joy. Let's
consider how joy is related to love and peace.

Those who have a version of joy without love can be very self-
centered and may lack empathy for others. You may know someone who appears joyful but their joy is shallow; they retain it by
being oblivious to the needs of others, clueless about the pain and
suffering around them. Their joy may even be at the expense of

others. I have known a few people like this, and they are not fun to be around. They often maintain their joy by shielding themselves from the pain of others. Troubling news rolls off them without effect. Joy is not just putting on a happy face, or being filled with irrepressible optimism in the face of pain and loss.

Similarly, peace without love and joy is a counterfeit peace. In the 1970s, as a campus minister, I watched students who were attending the Erhard Seminars Training weekends. They would pay good money for the experience of going away to be treated abusively, insulted, and forbidden to talk to fellow participants or go to the bathroom for hours at a time. The goal was apparently to experience a sort of peace or tranquility; even in the face of fearsome treatment, to remain cool and calm, unaffected, detached; to learn to control your emotions. Perhaps some people were helped by this, but what I saw were students who came back with a glassy-eyed, detached calmness, which is a counterfeit to real, biblical peace and joy. God's peace is not a tranquilizer.

Christian peace does not come from the annihilation of feelings and desires, which is more characteristic of Stoicism or the viewpoint of certain Eastern religions. Rather, peace can accompany the proper expression and fulfillment of our God-given desires. Similarly, God's gift of joy is not a passive denial of or resignation to the pain and unpleasant experiences of life, but rather an honest recognition and acceptance of this pain in light of God's goodness, mercy, and love. Passive, emotionless, detached peace is a poor substitute for the exciting expression of joy God intends for us.

As C. S. Lewis so eloquently states,

> It would seem that our Lord finds our desires not too strong, but too weak. We are half-hearted creatures, fooling about with drink and sex and ambition when infinite joy is offered us, like an ignorant child who wants to go on making mud pies in a

slum because he cannot imagine what is meant by the offer of a holiday at the sea. We are far too easily pleased.[12]

Another way of stating it is that our problem is not that we desire too much, but that we settle for so little. There is much talk these days about the dangers of *settling*, whether in choosing a marriage partner, or taking a job we really don't like. Our human tendency is also to settle for junk food, junk sex, junk pleasures, or any number of other cheap substitutes for the real thing. The real thing is finding joy in God's good gifts, according to his plan and purpose for these gifts.

We have seen how Jesus conveyed his peace to his disciples — "Peace I leave with you; my peace I give to you. Not as the world gives do I give to you" (John 14:27). This peace that Jesus gives is not dependent on world peace; it is beyond the reach of the tragic and the terrible. Paul later states that Jesus not only offers peace; he himself *is* our peace (Eph. 2:14). Commenting on this passage, Dr. Walter Wilson, a medical doctor in Missouri who later became a preacher, recalled the days when he used to make house calls as a doctor. Often, he would enter a home where a woman was in labor, about to give birth, or where someone was deathly ill. The whole house would be in a panic, and the people were desperate. Then he would enter and would hear people whisper, "The doctor is here; it's OK." And an amazing calm and peace came over that whole household. He remembered feeling unworthy of such trust, and at the same time a deep sense of responsibility. But his presence *was* their peace, and Jesus's presence *is* our peace.

And he *is* our joy. I have seen the power of prayer to turn panic into peace. When we call upon Jesus to enter even the most frightening state of affairs, something supernatural happens. We sense a calm. When I was a young pastor, a woman called our church for help. She had seen the movie *The Exorcist*, and she was terrified that she was under attack. As we prayed, she invited Jesus into her life. I watched a peace come over her. Then she beamed with joy. She suddenly realized that some sounds she was hearing were simply from a rusty gate. Later, as a campus minister, I saw this kind of transformation take place in the lives of scores of students, turning fear into peace and joy.

Joy as a By-Product

I have said that joy is a by-product, an outgrowth of something else. We don't find joy by pursuing joy; we find it by pursuing something else. But again, we might rightly ask, What is that something else? What is it that produces joy? In the New Testament, joy accompanies a right relationship with God through Jesus Christ, and the resultant right relationship with others. Christian joy emerges from a profound understanding of who God is and what he is about. It comes from an unshakable certainty of God's dramatic rescue plan for this world — to reconcile all things in heaven and earth in Christ (Eph. 1:10). It is a result of being indwelt by the Holy Spirit and allowing his fruit to grow and flourish through us. We don't get joy by trying harder. It is not achieved by straining, struggling, and striving. It is gained by resting in God's love and grace.

> Through him [Jesus] we have also obtained access by faith into this grace in which we stand, and we rejoice in hope of the glory of God. (Rom. 5:2)

> More than that, we also rejoice in God through our Lord Jesus Christ, through whom we have now received reconciliation. (Rom. 5:11)

> Though you have not seen him [Jesus], you love him. Though you do not now see him, you believe in him and rejoice with joy that is inexpressible and filled with glory. (1 Pet. 1:8)

As I noted earlier, Miroslav Volf at Yale University has been devoting a great deal of attention to redefining the "good life," and more particularly how the experience of joy is related to human flourishing. He contends that joy is not a self-standing emotion but the crown of a life well lived.

> Joy is not merely external to the good life, a mint leaf on the cake's whipped cream. Rather, the good life expresses and manifests itself in joy. Joy is the emotional dimension of a life that goes well and is led well.[13]

Brené Brown, in her best-selling book *Daring Greatly* and her popular TED Talks,[14] describes people who are "wholehearted." They are the people who are willing to take risks, to accept their vulnerability in the face of disappointment, uncertainty, and their own weakness. They are also the people who experience the most joy, creativity, courage, and gratitude in their lives. These conclusions follow thousands of interviews and surveys she, who has a PhD in social work, has conducted on the topic of shame and vulnerability.

But this still prompts the question, How do we lean into vulnerability? How do we come to the place of taking risks and living wholeheartedly, living this kind of fullness of life?

Jesus came that we might have life in all its fullness (John 10:10). Who wants to live a half-hearted life — a cautious, controlled, safe, fearful, and boring life? Jesus himself lived a full life, making himself vulnerable by entering into the hurts and heartaches and happiness of others he touched. He lived a generous life of giving himself away. He offers us life that is to be lived bravely, with an open heart, taking comfort in our dependence on God who loves us unconditionally. He calls his disciples to live life to the hilt, with loving and caring hearts, bringing comfort and healing to others. This is the life of joy, the good life, the flourishing life. This is what we were made for.

Chapter 2

Now that we have come to a better understanding of what joy is, we must turn our attention more fully to Jesus. For Jesus himself lived a joyful life, promised this joy to his disciples, and is the real joy-giver. Let's take another look, a fresh look, at who he really was and the effect he had on the people who encountered him.

When we consider the larger biblical picture, we can say that we were created for joy, but in our fallen condition, apart from God's grace, most people seldom attain that joyful state God intended for us and for which we yearn. In God's great redemptive plan, with the coming of Jesus, we have been given the means of recovering this experience of joy — genuinely, though not fully or continuously — in this life. And we are destined for a final, complete, uninterrupted joy in the land of love where there is no more sighing, crying, or dying, when we "enter into the joy of [our] master" (Matt. 25:21, 23; cf. Rev. 21).

Reflection Questions

1. What are some ways that you observe people trying to find happiness in your culture?

2. What do you think of Jesus's description of the "blessed" people, or truly joyful people (Matt. 5:3–12)? Which of these qualities are regularly a part of your life?

3. Sometimes we miss out on joy because we "settle" for so little. Are there areas in your life where you may have "settled" and missed out on the joy God intends for you?

4. If joy is a by-product and accompanies a right relationship with God through Jesus Christ, where are you on this journey?

3

Jesus, the Real Joy-Giver

When my son was about twelve, he asked me, "Dad, did Jesus ever tell a joke?" I couldn't come up with a joke. But it did start me thinking. What was Jesus like? I began to look more carefully at Jesus's interactions with people and the effect he had on them. I began to see humor in his teaching, in his parables, and an effervescence about him as he related to people. What is your general impression of Jesus? Do you envision him as stern, somber, dour, humorless, maybe even scary? If so, I want to invite you to reconsider your image of Jesus.

We are given very little information about the personality of Jesus in the Gospel accounts, and almost nothing about his physical appearance. This may be for good reason, given our human propensity to establish personality cults around famous people, and our track record of becoming enamored with celebrities. In today's culture we might be tempted to make Jesus into a superhero or an American Idol.

On the other hand, we can discover in the Gospels a great deal about Jesus's character and integrity, about his values and actions. We can view his interactions and conversations with individuals and groups of people. We can see the impact he had on the people who encountered him. We can also take note of the promises he made and the assurances he gave.

"My Joy Will Be in You"

Consider some of the promises Jesus made to his disciples. For example, in the Upper Room teaching, sometimes called the Farewell Discourse (John 13–17), Jesus is preparing his disciples for his departure and the events that will follow. He offers them tender reassurance and he makes promises, lots of promises.

- He promises not to leave them as orphans.
- He promises to send the Holy Spirit, the Comforter, the Paraclete (i.e., Advocate).
- He promises that they will see him again, after the Resurrection.
- He promises conflict with the world yet assures them that he has overcome the world.
- He promises to pass on his mission to them, to give them his words, his works, his power.
- He promises to answer their prayers in powerful ways.
- He promises to pass on his love – "As the Father has loved me, so I have loved you, and so you will love one another" (John 13:34).
- And he promises them *his* joy – "My joy will be in you, and your joy will be complete" (John 15:11 NIV).

From this evidence, and more to follow, we must conclude that Jesus was a joyful person and that he wanted his disciples to share this joy. I realize that may not be the first image that jumps into our minds about Jesus. In sermons and movies about him, we are often presented with a serious, ominous Jesus. But in fact, he was exceedingly generous, gentle, and compassionate. He especially welcomed the outcasts, the weak, and the afflicted. Children flocked to him. He continually brought joy into people's lives. Almost everyone who encountered Jesus came away happier and more fulfilled.

Jesus is not just saying, "You will have joy," but "*My* joy will be in you" (John 15:11). Again, in his prayer to the Father, Jesus says, "I am coming to you now, but I say these things while I am still in the world, so that they may have the full measure of *my* joy within them" (John 17:13, emphasis mine). Jesus possessed joy and emanated joy.

In the same way, he offers his disciples his peace — "My peace I give to you" (John 14:27). And he gives them his love. This wonderful trio of virtues — love, joy, and peace — is to characterize his followers. "By this all people will know that you are my disciples" (John 13:35).

Love, joy, and peace are the three qualities that most permeated the life and ministry of Jesus, and he passes them on to his disciples.

Jesus's Sense of Humor

A lot of us tend to overlook some of the humor in Jesus's teaching. Consider, for example, the part of his Sermon on the Mount where he describes how the hypocrites call attention to themselves when they give, pray, and fast:

> "Thus, when you give to the needy, sound no trumpet before you, as the hypocrites do in the synagogues and in the streets, that they may be praised by others. Truly, I say to you, they have received their reward." (Matt. 6:2)

Jesus paints a comical picture of the hypocritical religious leaders of the day standing on the street corner with their own personal trumpeter announcing their good deeds. I imagine the scene would look something like this:

"Hear ye, hear ye! *[The trumpet blasts.]* Rabbi Hillel will now contribute a very large donation for the poor. Let's have a big round of applause for this holy man of God!" *[More trumpet fanfare]*

Now, come on, this is funny! Whether Jesus is referring to literal trumpets or using a comedic device of hyperbole to get the point across, he is still using humor. As Jesus so vividly describes the absurdity of false piety, I picture the disciples rolling on the ground with gut-splitting laughter, because they recognize this familiar scene. But then there is the sober conclusion: those who flaunt their piety have received all the reward they will ever get. The laughing stops and the lesson is driven in deeply. There is nothing like laughter to open our hearts to receive an important truth.

In his book *What's So Funny About God?*, Steve Wilkens, a philosophy professor at Azusa Pacific University, suggests that perhaps the problem with many biblical scholars is that they "take humor too seriously."[1] If you don't believe God has a sense of humor, he says, just look in the mirror. Or, we might say, look at the elephant, on which God put the tail on the other end. Or the kiwi bird, the gooney bird landings, the rooster crowing, or the rhinoceros running. Ecclesiastes reminds us that "there is a time to laugh" (Eccles. 3:4). Dr. Edmund Clowney loved retelling the story about the time God told Sarah she would have a son in her old age, and she secretly laughed. When the angel confronted her about laughing, she denied it and said, "No, I didn't laugh." But the angel said, "Oh, but you did laugh" (see Gen. 18:10–15). And when their son was born, God told Abraham to name him Isaac, which means "laughter," so that — Dr. Clowney added — posterity would know God had the last laugh.

Jesus was fully human, which means that, among other things, he laughed. Donald Sweeting, president of Colorado Christian University, asks: Can you imagine Jesus at a dinner party and never laughing, or turning water into wine and not cracking a smile? His teachings are full of one-liners displaying irony, satire, and hyperbole. We find quips about straining gnats and swallowing camels, being concerned with the speck in your brother's eye and not the log in your own eye, and a camel going through the eye of a needle. In the comical parable of the rich fool, we are told that his barns were bulging with grain, so he built bigger barns and then told himself to relax and eat, drink, and be merry. But God told him, "Tonight you will die — then who will get all your stuff?"[2] The musical *Godspell* captures much of the humor in Jesus's parables.

Maybe we need to lighten up a bit in our reading of Scripture. Wilkens suggests that we consider again the story about the disciples on the road to Emmaus (Luke 24:13–35).[3] Jesus clearly "plays" these two disciples for a while as he suddenly joins them on the road. They do not recognize him. They are discussing the amazing things that have happened in Jerusalem about one Jesus of Nazareth. Jesus, apparently with a straight face, asks them what they are talking about. They respond, "Are you the only one who has not heard about these things?" Jesus responds, "What things?" Of course he knew what things. There must have been at least a twinkle in his eye by this time. This is at least Socratic irony. Of course, he doesn't leave them there. He later opens their eyes to see how the Scriptures spoke of him from the beginning.

The Joy of the Bridegroom

For his first miracle, Jesus turned water into wine (John 2:1–12). What kind of person starts a religion by throwing a party? In the first place, there he is, not by accident attending a wedding celebration. What kind of prophet is this, mingling with people's happiness? Then, when the fun is about to go out of the party, just when the hosts are about to be humiliated by running out of wine, Jesus comes to the rescue with a miraculous transformation, producing some very excellent wine. When the wedding planner tastes this new wine, he is amazed that the groom saved the best wine for last.

Elsewhere Jesus extends this wedding metaphor to his own relationship with his disciples, portraying himself as the bridegroom. When the Pharisees complain that Jesus's disciples are not fasting as their disciples are, Jesus responds, "Can the wedding guests fast while the bridegroom is with them? As long as they have the bridegroom with them, they cannot fast. The days will come when the bridegroom is taken away from them, and then they will fast in that day" (Mark 2:19–20). You don't fast when the bridegroom has arrived at the party. Jesus was present with them; it was time to celebrate.

John the Forerunner understood this reality when he said of Jesus, "The bride belongs to the bridegroom. The friend who attends the bridegroom waits and listens for him and is *full of joy* when he hears the bridegroom's voice. That joy is mine, and it is now complete" (John 3:29, emphasis mine). John identifies himself as the "friend" of the groom, perhaps the best man in this scenario, and his heart is full of joy because of his great privilege to witness the coming of the bridegroom.

Jesus's Joyful Ministry

People were drawn to Jesus, and they almost always left him overjoyed. Ironically, the notable exceptions to this pattern were the religious rulers. Because of their defensive posture and their desire to retain their position of power and prestige, the Pharisees, Sadducees, and scribes were baffled by him. Their encounters with Jesus left them confused, angry, and hostile. They missed out on the wonderful message of redemption and peace and joy that he was bringing into the world.

To the religious rulers, Jesus seemed to break all the rules. He was impertinent about fasting. He ignored the Sabbath laws. (Even *healing* on the Sabbath was considered a violation in their view!) And what was their most frequent accusation against Jesus? He hung out with sinners and tax collectors.

The problem is that Jesus didn't behave like a prophet at all. John the Baptist they could understand. They didn't like him, and they didn't accept his message, but they understood him. He dressed like a prophet, he ate like a prophet, he lived like a prophet. But this Jesus was far too sunny-hearted.

Here was Jesus going about interrupting funerals with his rude resurrections and throwing life into general disarray with his spoilsport healings and exorcisms. During one of Jesus's home sermons, a paralyzed man was lowered into the gathered crowd from an opening in the roof, and Jesus proceeded to heal him — after which the man leapt about in full view of everyone (Mark 2:1–12). Jesus even had the audacity to declare that the man's sins were forgiven, making himself out to be God. He appears to take great delight in bringing happiness to people in need, and is astonished at those who take offense.

For example, in John 9, Jesus encounters a man blind from birth. It was the Sabbath. The Pharisees were lurking about, waiting to see if he would heal the man, because surely no true prophet of God, and certainly no Messiah, would dare to heal a man on the Sabbath. In spite of this, Jesus, out of love and a desire to bring new joy into this man's life, heals the man's eyes. The Pharisees had now had enough! This Jesus was an imposter, a false prophet. But when they try to explain this to the healed man, he just says, "One thing I know, that though I was blind, now I see" (John 9:25). When they press him further, he says, "Why do you want to hear it again? Do you also want to become his disciples?" (John 9:27). Ouch! This man seems to have a greater sense of humor than the Pharisees. And a greater understanding of the truth.

Do we grasp the irony of this scene? Who is blind in this story and who is seeing? Instead of being joyful about this man's healing, the religious leaders are blinded by their preoccupation with Sabbath laws. It is their spiritual blindness that prevents the Pharisees from rejoicing over this blind man's good fortune. It is their spiritual blindness that keeps them in darkness about Jesus. They completely miss the deeper truth about Jesus, that he came as the light of the world (John 8:12; 9:5).

In John's Gospel, the seven "signs," or miracles, that are selected point to a larger truth about Jesus's identity and his mission in this world. He feeds the five thousand and declares, "I am the bread of life." He heals the blind man and announces, "I am the light of the world." He raises Lazarus from the dead and proclaims, "I am the resurrection and the life." And so these miracles are called "signs" because they signify a greater spiritual truth about Jesus. The drama in this section is riveting, and liberating, and so full of life and love and joy.

Jesus sums up the complaint of the religious rulers about himself in this statement:

"For John came neither eating nor drinking, and they say, 'He has a demon.' The Son of Man came eating and drinking, and they say, 'Look at him! A glutton and a drunkard, a friend of

tax collectors and sinners!' Yet wisdom is justified by her deeds."
(Matt. 11:18–19)

This statement, like so many others, is filled with satire. We might paraphrase it: "You were not impressed with John, the ascetic prophet, who came preaching in the wilderness. And yet you are not pleased with the Son of Man, who comes as the bridegroom, celebrating and mixing with the outcasts of society. You are very difficult people to please."

We see Jesus's lightheartedness in the passage where children are brought to him. He takes them up in his arms and lap and holds them, blesses them, and even uses them as an object lesson.

> And they were bringing children to him that he might touch them, and the disciples rebuked them. But when Jesus saw it, he was indignant and said to them, "Let the children come to me; do not hinder them, for to such belongs the kingdom of God. Truly, I say to you, whoever does not receive the kingdom of God like a child shall not enter it." And he took them in his arms and blessed them, laying his hands on them. (Mark 10:13–16)

Children are not attracted to scary people, but to warm, inviting, smiling people.

As I have said, people who encountered Jesus almost always went away happy. Not only the people he healed and delivered from evil spirits, though they certainly were jubilant, but others (like many of us) who were forgiven, enlightened, and set free. The Samaritan woman was ecstatic to finally find not just water, but that for which her soul truly thirsted. She had met the Messiah and she went and told everyone about it. Nicodemus was freed from his religiosity the night he met Jesus and later became a disciple. Mary

Magdalene received a new lease on life, being delivered from seven demons. The woman who washed Jesus's feet with her tears was "forgiven much" and went away transformed.

Jesus came to Jericho and invited himself over to Zacchaeus's house for dinner (Luke 19:1–10). I have always liked that about Jesus. "I am coming to your house today." Poor Zacchaeus, who had climbed a tree just to get a glimpse of Jesus, must have practically fallen out of the tree. He was a tax collector, despised by everyone. He had been cheating his fellow Jews for years, lining his own pockets with their money. But we are told that Zacchaeus "welcomed [Jesus] gladly." The other Jews in the city were aghast. And apparently, no sooner had Jesus entered his house than Zacchaeus began to repent of his sins, promising to pay back any he had cheated, fourfold. We don't know what conversation they may have had over dinner. But in conclusion Jesus says, "Today, salvation has come to this house, since he also is a son of Abraham. For the Son of Man came to seek and to save the lost" (Luke 19:9–10). Zacchaeus was saved from his own greed, set free from the prison he had made for himself, liberated to live, to love, and to serve. And no doubt, for the first time in a very long time, Zacchaeus felt true joy.

One of the few people who went away sad from a conversation with Jesus was the rich young ruler. He asks Jesus, "What must I do to inherit eternal life?" Jesus recites the commandments. The man says, "All these I have kept since I was a boy." Jesus's next words seem shocking and have raised many questions from commentators, but he knew the man's heart and what it was that enslaved him. "'One thing you still lack. Sell all that you have and distribute to the poor, and you will have treasure in heaven; and come, follow me.' But when he heard these things, he became very sad, for he was extremely rich. Jesus, seeing that he had become sad, said, 'How difficult it is for those who have wealth to enter the kingdom of God!'" (Luke 18:22–24).

This story has always left me with an aching in my heart for this man. He did not realize the great prize that was being offered to him — the kingdom of God, which was worth far more than all his riches. We might think back to the parable of the treasure in the field. When the man found this treasure, "in his joy, he went away and sold everything he had and bought that field" (Matt. 13:46). Jesus offers people a greater joy, a greater reward that far outweighs everything else we might prize.

I remember hearing a story of a homeless man in Chicago who approached a man for money. The man he approached was part of the Jesus People community. He said to the homeless man, "I can give you a few dollars, but if you come with me, I will offer you much more, a whole new life, food and a place to live, and the warmth of a caring community." The man took the few dollars and went away sad because he could not fathom the great gift he was being offered.

The rich young ruler represents so many who cling to the security of their own lives, whatever it may be, and miss out on the great offer of all-surpassing joy. And sometimes the story reminds me of, well, *me*, when I settle for the poor substitutes of money, fame, reputation, pride, and little pleasures instead of embracing the pure, sweet joy offered by Jesus. "Blessed are the pure in heart, for they shall see God" (Matt. 5:8). This is the greater joy we are offered — to see God.

In my imagination I sometimes try to look into the hearts of the people surrounding Jesus during his earthly life to try to understand the depth of their feelings, to try to envision what had happened to them as a result of their encounter with Jesus. I have written soliloquies in the voice of some of these figures.

One of them is Mary Magdalene. We don't know much about Mary's history. She encountered Jesus in her hometown of Magdala,

and we are told that "seven demons came out of her" (Luke 8:2).
There is some speculation that she might have been a prostitute. We
cannot be sure, but in the following story I will make that assumption. After her transformative encounter with Jesus, she became part
of a group of women who left their homes and traveled with Jesus and
the disciples. She was also present at the crucifixion and was the first
person to see Jesus after his resurrection. What *is* clear is that her life
was dramatically turned around and she became a devoted follower
of Jesus to the end. Jesus had given her back her life. What joy!

What was she thinking in the dark hours of the first Easter
morning as she approached the tomb where Jesus was buried? The
following soliloquy is based on the John 20 narrative.

Mary's Story

*How could I not visit his tomb that morning? He had given me back my life.
I had waited impatiently all Sabbath. We could not visit the tomb on the Sabbath. So, very early the next morning — it was still dark — I began the long walk
to the grave where I knew they had laid his body.*

As I walked, I remembered.

*How well I remember when the Teacher first came to Magdala. He taught
with such authority, but he was so gentle. And the healings! My, how he healed
so many — the sick, the paralyzed, the blind, the leprous! I kept in the shadows
and away from this man. I did not understand him. He was not like any man I
had known before. And I had known many men. I took their money and gave
them pleasure. Yes, I was a harlot. I was a mockery in my own town. I say it with
shame now, but at that time it seemed to be the only choice I had. I felt trapped
in the miserable cycle of sex for money, looking for intimacy, and I only became
more and more lonely and bitter. People just thought I was crazy.*

*Then came that day that changed my whole life. He spotted me in the
crowd. He singled me out. I knew I had been found out. I wanted to hide. Some-*

thing inside me made me want to run. At the same time, I wanted so desperately to be delivered from this terrible prison of my pathetic existence. He reached toward me and said something. I covered my ears and froze in panic. I heard the words — "Come out from her."

I am not sure what happened next. People said my whole body began to convulse, to shake, and with a shudder I fell to the ground. They thought I was dead. But Jesus came to me and took my hand and lifted me up. I looked into his eyes, so kind, so full of love. I will never forget it. I felt like I had just been born, that I had just begun to live. I felt so peaceful. Everything around me looked different — the colors, the sounds, the people, the sky. I never knew it could be like this.

They said seven demons came out of me. All I know is I felt free for the first time since I could remember. I felt lighter, like I might float away. I looked at him. He was looking back. Everyone was looking at me. He gave me back my life that day.

After that, I followed him. Where else could I go? There were other women, like me, who had been delivered. We followed him, along with his disciples. As I listened to his amazing teaching about this new kingdom, I could feel my heart swell within me. I drank in his words. I watched with the others as he continued to heal and deliver so many others. I told everyone who would listen about how he set me free.

The days went on. Sometimes I felt my heart would burst with joy. To think that someone like me could feel so clean, so pure, so alive — it still amazes me to this day. I loved him and love him still; not like I had ever loved anyone before. I knew that I would sacrifice everything for him. I would gladly lay down my life.

He also had enemies. The religious leaders seemed to hate him, to fear him. They followed him around. They wanted to trick him, to stop him, to silence him. I could not understand why everyone would not open their hearts to him and receive his wonderful teaching. It was so good and true. But the opposition grew.

Chapter 3

Then the day came that I had dreaded. They took him away and accused him of all sorts of fabricated crimes. I could see where this was going. But surely, he would stop it. I had seen the kind of power he had. I was sure he would put an end to it. But he didn't! They beat him and sentenced him to die. They led him outside Jerusalem with that terrible cross. I watched. I stayed and watched everything. How could I leave? Where could I go? But he didn't stop them! They nailed him to that awful cross and I watched him hang there in agony. Once, he looked straight down at me. I am sure of it. No words. Just those same eyes — now full of sadness, full of pain, but still somehow expressing love and hope. It was like he wanted me to understand something. But then I watched him die. My heart broke. It seemed like my life had ended. I followed to where they took him — to Joseph's tomb. I would be back to mourn, to anoint him for burial.

I waited all day that Sabbath in a gloomy state of confusion. I still had the new life he had given me, but they had taken my Lord from me. So I made my way to the tomb before dawn on Sunday. When I arrived, I was shocked and confused to see the stone rolled away and the tomb empty. I had hoped to find at least some consolation in anointing his body and mourning for him with the other women. Now they had even taken that away from me. But as I looked again in the tomb, I was amazed to see two men in dazzling brightness, sitting where his body had been. My amazement was growing by the minute.

"Why are you crying?" they asked me.

"Why am I crying? They have taken away my Lord" was all I could get out. "First they crucified my Lord, and now they have taken his body and robbed me of any consolation."

Then I heard someone behind me. I turned around and saw another man, strangely familiar, but I wasn't sure why. He asked me the same question: "Why are you crying?"

Why do they keep asking me this question? I thought he must be the gardener or some official. "Sir, if you have carried him away, just tell me where you have put him, and I will get him." I tried to sound confident.

Then he looked at me with great compassionate eyes and simply said, "Mary." Oh, I knew that voice. Only he spoke my name in that way. But my mind must be playing tricks on me. It can't be. I saw him die. But here he is standing in front of me. How could I not have recognized him? My heart began to swell with joy as the realization of this fact began to dawn on me. He's alive! Here he is! I should have known that death could not hold him. Oh, how stupid I have been. Of course he's alive. Of course his body was not in the tomb.

I fell at his feet and said, "Rabboni" — my own dear Teacher. That was what I called him. Now my tears of joy were falling on his feet. I clutched at his feet. I never wanted to let go.

But he lifted me up and said I should bring the news to his disciples. What was I thinking? Of course, I must tell them. This news is not just for me. I did not want to leave him, ever again, but I had to go. I started to run, then I stopped and looked back, then ran on. I wanted to say, "Don't move. Stay right there." He just smiled at me with great assurance.

So I ran all the way to the house where they were staying. I was out of breath and excited and could hardly get the words out — "I have seen the Lord!" They sat me down, and I told them the whole story.

Yes, Jesus is the real joy-giver. He himself, in his time on this earth, possessed a deep and abiding joy. He promises to give *us* that joy. He fervently wants us to have it. Many of us have tasted of his joy. It is sweet and pure. It fills our soul. It is good. It makes us feel truly alive. It is life, in all its fullness.

At the same time, on this side of glory, joy seems to be a fleeting thing. Many voices, distractions, and temptations compete for our attention and devotion, leading us away from joy. There are enemies of joy, forces that would steal our joy every time.

But there is joy in knowing Jesus. There is joy in following Jesus. There is joy in serving Jesus, the kind of joy that can be found nowhere else.

Chapter 3

But what do we do if we have lost the joy? Can we find it again? Read on.

Reflection Questions

1. Do you think of Jesus as a joyful person? How have you changed your view on this as you reflect on his life and ministry?
2. What was it about Jesus that made the religious rulers so angry and hostile?
3. Consider some of the people who encountered Jesus and went away overwhelmed with joy — the Samaritan woman, Zacchaeus, Mary Magdalene. Can you place yourself in their lives and imagine how you would have responded?
4. Have you had an experience like that of Mary Magdalene, where you might say of Jesus, "He gave me back my life"?

4

Where Is This Joy to Be Found?

The announcement came over the PA system at the ballpark. "Attention. For the man who lost a large wad of twenty-dollar bills in a rubber band: we have found your rubber band." OK, it's a joke.

But now for a true story. One day our son found a diamond ring, just inside the sewer drain on the side of the road near our house. We thought and prayed as a family about what to do with it. Finally we decided to print notices about the ring and take them around to our neighbors. We asked that if anyone had lost a ring and could describe it, to please contact us. The woman two doors down called us and described the ring in perfect detail. She was ecstatic to have found her lost wedding ring. And we were happy to see her so joyful.

Lost and Found

This incident reminds me of a story Jesus told, a parable about a woman who lost a silver coin. She was so distraught that she lit a lamp and swept the whole house until she finally found that coin. Then she invited her neighbors over to celebrate. "Rejoice with me," she said. "I have found my lost coin" (Luke 15:8–10). But Jesus was really talking about lost people being found.

Jesus spoke of finding joy. But he also spoke of the joy of being found by God. It is through his parables — real-life stories that pack a wallop — that Jesus unfolds this great truth most fully.

In his parables in Matthew 13, Jesus presents the kingdom as the great prize we didn't even know we were seeking. It is a wonderful surprise that we almost stumble upon. We may have thought we were looking for something else, something less exciting, and then *eureka!* There it is, right in front of our noses. But when we find it, really find it, we realize its immeasurable worth. Nothing else in life compares to this great prize. Not even close. That is why it is said, "The kingdom of heaven is like treasure hidden in a field. When a man found it, he hid it again, and then in his joy went and sold all he had and bought that field" (Matt. 13:44).

The point of these parables, of course, is not that this prize, the kingdom of heaven, can be bought. The point is that it is priceless. It is far beyond anything we could imagine. And, of course, to discover the kingdom is to also find Jesus, the King. To enter his kingdom brings us joy, joy, joy! Our hearts well up so much that they are about to burst.

I worked at youth camps and college-age camps at different times in my life. And every camp must have a "lost and found" box or room. If a camper has lost an item, the first thing to do is look in the lost-and-found box. Perhaps some dear person found it lying around and placed it in the box. And what a great joy and relief it is for us to find our lost item there.

When it comes to people who are "lost and found," Jesus has three "lost" parables to tell: the lost sheep, the lost coin, and the lost son (or the two lost sons). All three are full of rejoicing:

- "Rejoice with me, for I have found my sheep that was lost." (Luke 15:6)

- "Rejoice with me, for I have found the coin that I had lost." (Luke 15:9)
- "It was fitting to celebrate and be glad, for this your brother was dead, and is alive; he was lost, and is found." (Luke 15:32)

And in each of these three parables there is great joy. There is joy on the part of Jesus who does the finding, or the Father who welcomes home his lost son. There is rejoicing on the part of the angels in heaven "over one sinner who repents" (Luke 15:7, 10). There is certainly joy on the part of the prodigal son who was lost but now is found.

Earl Palmer speaks of the element of surprise, saying, "That whimsical, celebrative laughter of heaven is the best surprise of all in these parables. It is not laughter at our expense, but the laughter of thankful enjoyment for the costly love of the waiting father who makes each son welcome by taking upon himself each one's lostness, disarming its anger and despair."[1]

How often have we seen paintings of Jesus having left the ninety-nine sheep in the field to seek and find the one that was lost, now carrying the one lost sheep on his shoulders, in a storm, along rocky cliffs, bringing it home to safety? I recently heard a story of a woman who knew very little about the Christian faith, but hearing the story of the lost sheep, she suddenly cried out, "That is me! I am the lost sheep." And she came to faith in Christ. It is a story that resonates deeply with us. That feeling of being lost and alone, scared, cold, shivering — then suddenly the Rescuer appears and carries us home. Jesus, and all of heaven, is throwing a party, rejoicing over that one woman who was lost but now is found.

Can we let ourselves join in that heavenly party? Can we lift up our hearts in rejoicing when we witness or hear of someone who was lost being found? After thirty-five years of campus ministry with college students, people often ask me, "What is your greatest joy?" I have three. First is the joy of seeing someone come to faith in Jesus, and having the privilege of hearing their first-ever prayer, something like, "Well God, I don't really know how to talk to you, but here goes . . ." I have heard many such prayers. My second greatest joy is introducing students to the Scriptures in a way that they can read them and understand them and apply them for themselves, feeding themselves from God's word. We call this "inductive Bible study." My third greatest joy is having a part in developing students as Christian leaders — seeing the transformation of a scared, green, reluctant young leader into a strong, visionary, spiritual leader for God. And not only have *I* rejoiced again and again in witnessing these supernatural transformations, but I believe that Jesus and the angels in heaven are overflowing with joy with each of these miracles.

As for my own conversion experience, it is hard to describe how I was drawn to God and Christ. In one sense, I was seeking something more. In another, it seemed that God was drawing me further in. Looking back on it now, I can see there were surprising events in which God was preparing me to receive his grace. It felt more as though I was found by God. I can identify with the anonymous nineteenth-century hymn writer who penned these lines:

> I sought the Lord, and afterward I knew
> He moved my soul to seek him, seeking me.
> It was not I that found, O Savior true;
> No, I was found of Thee.[2]

My Journey to Faith and Joy

I became a believer at age eighteen, after a time of searching. I took a year off between high school and college to earn some money and do some traveling (hitchhiking through Mexico and crossing the Caribbean on a shrimp boat . . . but that is another story). I was ready to give up on religion, concluding that it was just for children and old people, certainly not for thinking people like me. I was following a somewhat pagan lifestyle — not wild, but self-seeking. But a strange thing happened to me on the way to becoming an atheist, as my older brother had already done. I encountered the real thing. And it came in the form of a small country church, with a very genuine pastor, filled with people who really knew God, who worshipped with a genuine love for God, who read the Bible like they really believed it, and who prayed as though God was really there. Simple people, not particularly charismatic, but authentic believers, and joyful. The real deal.

This led me to take another look at Christian faith, to reconsider. I found that I wanted to be around these people. There was something attractive about them. Yes, there was a joy in their lives that was appealing and delightful. I began asking questions, raising my objections and doubts, but gradually my resistance began to weaken. I got into a home Bible study with the parents of a close high school friend of mine. The joy of the gospel was contagious in that home. The simple message of the gospel — Jesus's life, sacrificial death, and resurrection — took hold of my mind and heart. I remember writing out John 3:16, and writing my name in place of the "whoever." For the first time, I realized that the gospel story calls for a response. After a period of months, and with the help of the pastor of that church, I finally yielded to the Lordship of Jesus, laid my sins out before him, and received his glorious forgiveness and the gift of new life. Like Christian in *The Pilgrim's Progress*, I felt the burden of sin roll off of my back. I felt so free and so light that I was afraid I might float away. I was glad that my car was holding me to the road during my trip home that night at 2 a.m.

During that time I was working to make money for college in a factory in Chicago, near Wrigley Field. And because my newfound faith was so fresh and exciting, I took my lunch hours to go up on the factory rooftop, to be alone and to sing the few Christian songs that I knew. I sang at the top of my lungs, with tears streaming down my face. And I was filled with joy. "Amazing grace, how sweet the sound." Yes!

If you are a believer, do you remember? Can you recall when you first discovered the joy of Christ and his kingdom? Or perhaps you grew up in a Christian home, but there was a time when God became real to you, delivered you, met you in a time of need? There is joy in knowing Jesus.

It is true that over time, the joy begins to fade. Our new life becomes ho-hum as the newness wears off. But the joy is not gone. We find that it is easily refreshed and resurfaces. We might see a double rainbow, or a gorgeous sunset. It might be a walk in the woods, hearing the crisp, bright song of a cardinal. We may be moved to tears by listening to Mozart's Requiem, or by joining with the saints in worship. We are dumbstruck again by sins forgiven, God's mercy new for this morning, or a Scripture passage speaking to us personally.

Even when we are having a bad day, we live in the truth of the gospel, in the thrill of knowing Jesus. Ben Patterson comments that he now responds differently to the polite question "How are you doing, Ben?" He often answers with "Well, other than the fact that my sins are completely forgiven, and I am guaranteed eternity with God forever, I'm not doing very well."[3]

A Rivendell on Lake Michigan

I suspect that there is in every heart a longing for joy, a desire for something that transcends the ordinariness of life. Whether you consider yourself a religious person or not, there may linger in the deepest reaches of your soul the ache for something just out of reach, something hard to define, outside of yourself, something absolutely beautiful and good and warm and loving.

During the Christmas season there is often this sense of wonder and awe in the air. There are the carols, the bells, the hustle and bustle of gift buying, maybe the purity of freshly fallen snow, the glistening lights, the food and drink, the gathering of friends around the fire, the magic of Santa and stockings and glowing Christmas trees. Love is in the air. It stirs in even the hardest of hearts. We begin to feel a fresh wave of joy, but we can't quite grasp it.

J. R. R. Tolkien captures this mood in his description of Rivendell in *The Fellowship of the Ring*, the house of Elrond, where the hobbits and their companions pause along their journey for shelter, safety, refreshment, and healing.

> Elrond's house was "perfect, whether you liked food or sleep or story-telling or singing (or reading), or just sitting and thinking best, or a pleasant mixture of them all." . . .
>
> "It's a big house this, and very peculiar. Always a bit more to discover, and no knowing what you'll find round a corner. And Elves, sir! Elves here, and Elves there! Some like kings, terrible and splendid; and some as merry as children. And the music and the singing . . ."
>
> "[There is] the Hall of Fire, . . . [where] you will hear many songs and tales — if you can keep awake. But except on high days it usually stands empty and quiet, and people come here who wish for peace, and thought. There is always a fire here, all the year round, but there is little other light." . . .
>
> "Time doesn't seem to pass here: it just is. A remarkable place altogether. . . ."

For a while the hobbits continued to talk and think of the past journey and of the perils that lay ahead; but such was the virtue of Rivendell that soon all fear and anxiety was lifted from their minds. The future, good or ill, was not forgotten, but ceased to have any power over the present.[4]

The hobbits are mesmerized by their sojourn at Rivendell. There is something magical about the place, and a timelessness. They are transfixed by the warmth, safety, merriment, music, conversation, and good friendship. They don't want to leave, but they have to go back into the world to continue their dangerous mission with the Ring.

My wife and I have had a tradition of gathering for a New Year's Eve dinner and celebration with friends, about twenty-five to thirty of us at a large house on Lake Michigan belonging to one of our friends. Most of us spend the night and share breakfast the next morning. With the fireplace glowing, we enjoy plenty of good food and drink, lively conversation, the sharing of music and poetry, the reading of Psalm 90 to remember our mortality and God's faithfulness, and finally the singing of "Auld Lang Syne" with champagne at midnight. I have sometimes remarked that this is our Rivendell. For a few hours we experience something magical, something beyond this world — warmth, safety, friendship, and sheer joy. It stirs something deep within us. It is a taste of that which is to come. As I pause to look around at the faces shining with the flickering light from the fireplace, I see faces of joy and contentment and peace, kindred spirits who share a common mission in life, though with many differing roles to play.

And this is just a taste of what is yet to come. That is because we are destined for joy.

Reflection Questions

1. Jesus portrays his kingdom as a great treasure that is to be found. When we do, it gives us great joy. Do you think you have found this treasure? And does it bring you incomparable joy?
2. Finding Christ's kingdom, or salvation, is viewed as a surprise in his parables (e.g., the pearl of great price, treasure hidden in a field, the lost sheep that is found, the prodigal son who returns home). It doesn't seem to be what people are looking for or expect. What are most people looking for?
3. We have this seeming paradox that the kingdom is something we find, but we are found by Christ. How does this compare to your own experience?
4. Often, when we first come to Christ by faith, we are euphoric, filled with joy. But in time that initial joy begins to fade. Where are you on this spectrum? What experiences restore your joy when it has grown dull?

5

Rediscovering Childlike Joy

Most of us adults have learned to leave our childhood behind, with all its silliness, naivete, and self-centeredness. But there is a big difference between being *childish* and being *childlike*. Yes, we should hope to outgrow our childish attitudes and behavior, our thinking that the world revolves around us. But to lose our childlikeness is tragic. It means that some part of us, an important part, has died. It is the loss of wonder, the expression of sheer joy at the simplest things, the ability to laugh at ourselves, and a willingness to look foolish without feeling shame.

> Then children were brought to him that he might lay his hands on them and pray. The disciples rebuked the people, but Jesus said, "Let the little children come to me and do not hinder them, for to such belongs the kingdom of heaven." And he laid his hands on them and went away. (Matt. 19:13–15)

At another, even more serious level, losing our childlikeness can make us unable to receive the kingdom of God. What did Jesus mean, for example, by using children as an object lesson to characterize those who are fit for the kingdom? Surely it is because they are not proud and self-righteous; they are humble and "poor in spirit" (Matt. 5:3). Little children recognize their need and dependency. They are also very *trusting*, and this may be the key. They are not looking to their own resources for survival or security. It is noteworthy that this teaching about children is followed by the sad story of the rich young ruler, which is about how it is hard for the rich to enter God's kingdom.

George MacDonald said about his writings, "I write, not for children, but for the child-like, whether they be of five, or fifty, or seventy-five."[1] Indeed, MacDonald's writings are filled with a sort of levity and lightness of being, a carefree spirit. "MacDonald's concept of the 'childlike' reverberates throughout every work of his poetry, fiction, and non-fiction."[2] MacDonald himself was a winsome, fun-loving character, with a flair for the dramatic. At one time, when his family was in need of money, he packed up several of his eleven children and took to the road, performing family renditions of *The Pilgrim's Progress* from town to town, receiving offerings along the way. He formed deep and influential friendships with Lewis Carroll, G. K. Chesterton, and Oswald Chambers, and during his 1872–73 lecture tour in the United States, he won the friendship of Henry Wadsworth Longfellow, Walt Whitman, and even Mark Twain. His writings had a profound influence on C. S. Lewis, J. R. R. Tolkien, Madeleine L'Engle, and countless others. It is the unpretentious and childlike nature of his writings that makes them so endearing and joy-producing.

Have you ever watched a child who is completely lost in play, just bubbling up with joy so that he cannot contain it? It may be when he catches that first big fish, or when she wants to go really high on the swing. We see unrestrained joy that squeals with delight. Or maybe the child is completely absorbed in *serious* play, building a sandcastle on the beach or a fort out of sticks in the woods. Chesterton speaks of the paradox of "the gravity of a child at play."³ Nietzsche wrote that maturity consists in having rediscovered the seriousness one had as a child at play.

Most adults are not good at being childlike. We tend to be quite suspicious of unexamined exuberance. We are reluctant to display excessive joy for fear of being judged as childish or not being taken seriously. We make every effort to avoid looking foolish. Many of us would do well to rediscover aspects of the child in us. I am reminded of these lines from a Bob Dylan song: "People tell me it's a crime / To feel too much at any one time / All it cost me was a dime / But the bells refused to ring."⁴ Is it really a crime to feel too much joy?

As I said at the beginning of this book, it does not come easy for me to step into this childlike state of being. I am getting better at it, thanks to my grandchildren and my love of music. I can slip into being a "control freak" at times. This is an unhappy inclination to have in an imperfect world that has a tendency to swing out of control on a regular basis. Many of us are prone to worry and are often crippled by our fears. We are too often caught up in the frenetic lifestyle of the "adult world." We may look at a child lost in play with a sense of longing — "When did I lose that capacity?" Or we may respond more cynically — "One day he will wake up to the reality and hardship of life."

Lessons from the Children

My family and I have been longtime fans of A. A. Milne's *Winnie the Pooh* books. Some of us even visited the original "One Hundred Acre Wood" in East Sussex, playing Poohsticks on the bridge over the creek. We have reread these stories again and again (now to my grandchildren) because they contain some of the most important life lessons — lessons of friendship, of working together to solve a problem, and of navigating various personality types (Eeyore, Tigger, and everyone in between). And they remind us of that childlike joy we may have lost along the way.

In the 2018 movie *Christopher Robin*, starring Ewan McGregor, we find Christopher now as an adult. He has left the stuffed-animal friends of his childhood, who once seemed so real to him, far behind. He is now caught up in his career and has become absorbed in the pressures of work. He is haggard, hassled, and harassed. We see him neglecting his wife and children. He suddenly and shockingly meets up with his old childhood friend, that lovable bear Winnie the Pooh, who needs Christopher Robin to help him find his other friends. In doing so, Winnie helps Christopher to remember the simple joys of life. Along this adventure, Christopher rediscovers his lost childhood, regaining his sense of creativity and imagination, which even helps solve his most troubling work-related dilemma and ultimately makes him a much better husband, father, and employee. The lesson is clear: as the responsibilities of adult life begin to weigh us down, we need to recover that childlike part of us that reminds us how to laugh and play and really enjoy life.

You may remember the book *Children's Letters to God*.[5] It sold over one million copies and came out in several editions. Here are some of my favorite letters:

Dear God, Did you mean for the giraffe to look like that or was it an accident?

Dear God, I went to this wedding and they kissed right in church. Is that okay?

Dear God, I read where Thomas Edison made light. But we read in Sunday School you did. I bet he stole your idea.

Chapter 5

Dear God, I think about you sometimes even when I am not praying.

Dear God, I don't think anybody could be a better God. Well, I just want you to know that I am not just saying that because you are God.

Some others make mention of the disciples they like best, or showing off their new clothes in church. So, being the academic type that I am, I have, of course, done a careful analysis of these letters to try to figure out why they are so funny and delightful to us. It seems to me that they display a freshness, an innocence, and have a surprising simplicity about them. They are pure and honest, uninhibited, with unbounded expectation and unspoiled imagination. And most importantly, they lack the jaded view of life that tends to creep in later as we "mature."

Learning to Play

Let's face it. Some of us need to lighten up a bit, and not take ourselves quite so seriously. As I said, my grandchildren are helping me along this path. My five-year-old granddaughter sometimes invites me to join her for a tea party, which she has all set up for us. We sit on the floor, in serious play, with our imaginations running wild, lost in our make-believe world, with a sense of timelessness. We play in this state for a while, then suddenly she is done, and ready to move on to something else. I am always startled at this because I am not sure that I was ready to move on.

One summer my family was spending the month at a Christian student camp in Michigan's Upper Peninsula on the gorgeous coast of Lake Huron. One sunny afternoon our son, who was about six at the time, wanted to play at the Lake Huron beach. It was a short walk from the main camp. Our colleague Frank offered to supervise him. Our son hit the beach running, and began digging trenches, making rivers and pools, changing the direction of the water on the sand, and creating hills and valleys, totally lost in his own world. Finally, four hours later, Frank said, "It is getting close to dinnertime, and we should probably start the walk back to camp."

When they arrived at dinner, Frank was beaming with a big smile, saying, "What a gift, what a gift." To my questioning look, Frank said, "It seems so rare to see a child at that age who can entertain himself for four hours in a stretch. I sat on the picnic bench and studied him the whole time. He was totally caught up in his own imagination, oblivious to time, playing and building, and rebuilding. It was a joy for me just to watch him."

Child psychologists and educators regularly stress the importance of play in a child's development. Children learn by playing. In his landmark book *All I Really Need to Know I Learned in Kindergarten*, Robert Fulghum makes the case that in kindergarten we gain all the essentials of life.[6] It may be an overstatement, but he makes an important point. In kindergarten we learn how to get along with other people, not to hit, to play fair, to share, to take a nap, to clean up after ourselves, to laugh and cry, and so much more. In playing, we develop our imagination, our loves, our hopes and dreams. "Play is important because it provides a primary foundation for learning, exploring, problem-solving, and building an understanding of the world and your role within it."[7] Play is also essential for adults. Recent studies confirm that play reduces stress and increases learning.[8]

When we juxtapose play and learning, or play and work, we are perpetuating a false dichotomy. Playing is one of the ways we learn. And it can be difficult to distinguish play from work when we are really enjoying our work.

Chapter 5

Resting in the Father's Arms

We also learn some important features of a childlike posture by considering Jesus's example and his teaching in the Sermon on the Mount.

In the relationship between Jesus and the Father, George Mac-Donald finds a paradigm for the childlike:

> This relationship is above all rooted in trust and love. . . . Jesus' perfect trust in the Father means that he is also perfectly at home in the world and can move about it with a sort of light mobility, for the world is the Father's. Because of this complete trust in the Father, the true child is in harmony with all of God's creation. Rather than a heavy struggling with nature to provide for one's needs, the child has a sense of supreme liberty and lightness and can play and delight in all of the Father's works. He exists in a state of "divine carelessness."[9]

When Jesus spoke to his disciples in his great Sermon, he invited them to enter a very different kind of life, to orient themselves to an upside-down kingdom. He reminded them that they too have a heavenly Father who cares for them and knows their needs. Most surprisingly, he invited them into a life without worry, anxiety, or fear.

I am going to ask you to consider these familiar words of Jesus with a fresh look and an open heart:

> "Therefore I tell you, do not worry about your life, what you will eat or drink; or about your body, what you will wear. Is not life more than food, and the body more than clothes? Look at the birds of the air; they do not sow or reap or store away in barns, and yet *your heavenly Father* feeds them. Are you not much more

valuable than they? Can any one of you by worrying add a single hour to your life?

"And why do you worry about clothes? See how the flowers of the field grow. They do not labor or spin. Yet I tell you that not even Solomon in all his splendor was dressed like one of these. If that is how God clothes the grass of the field, which is here today and tomorrow is thrown into the fire, will he not much more clothe you — you of little faith? So do not worry, saying, 'What shall we eat?' or 'What shall we drink?' or 'What shall we wear?' For the pagans run after all these things, and *your heavenly Father* knows that you need them. But seek first his kingdom and his righteousness, and all these things will be given to you as well. Therefore do not worry about tomorrow, for tomorrow will worry about itself. Each day has enough trouble of its own." (Matt. 6:25–34 NIV, emphasis mine)

Doesn't this sound a lot like the childlike life? A carefree life? Notice the references to "your heavenly Father." Jesus lived this kind of life himself, knowing (as MacDonald noted) that he had a loving, eternal Father who cared for him and knew his needs, a Father who rules the world. He knew he could entrust himself completely to this loving Father. There was no need to worry or to be anxious. Yes, he was going to suffer and die, but not apart from the Father's knowledge and care.

This is the real key to living the childlike life of joy that Jesus intends for us: trust. If these promises are true — if our Father is truly all-powerful, fully loving and caring, and completely aware of our needs — then we can rest in his care. He is trustworthy. We can run to him in our time of need.

But so often we don't. We run in every other direction, any other direction, for help and solutions. We worry, we fret, we ag-onize, we panic, we scheme, we take control, or we give up in despair. I admit it. I often find myself trying to imagine every possible calamity that might befall me or those I love. This then leads me to imagine every possible way I might preempt those things from happening. And, of course, I can't. So do I fret, or do I trust? Of course, all the worrying and fretting is useless, a waste of time and energy and a thief of joy.

On another occasion, Jesus added these words, "Are not two sparrows sold for a penny? Yet not one of them will fall to the ground outside your Father's care. And even the very hairs of your head are all numbered. So don't be afraid; you are worth more than many sparrows" (Matt. 10:29–31). But, we may say, "Yes, but the sparrow does fall. How can we count on God to protect us? He can't guarantee that my child won't get hurt." Yes, but nothing happens outside the Father's care and knowledge.

Do you see how radical this teaching is? Can we entrust even our life, and the lives of our loved ones, to God's care? It may seem counterintuitive for us adults to trust unequivocally in this way. We generally live under the illusion that we actually can control our lives, and our death, if we try hard enough. Can we relinquish this imagined control of our lives that we never really had anyway? This is not a call to a careless, irresponsible life; it is an invitation to not worry and fret over those things we can't control.

There is no getting around it. The mind-boggling truth is that Jesus wants his disciples to live a life free from anxiety and fear. Jesus is the joy-giver, and he doesn't want us to live a fearful life. He wants us to live a life that is free and full and attuned to the present. We can't worry and be joyful at the same time. Worry is essentially a faith problem — "O you of little faith." It is a refusal or an inability to trust.

Have you ever gone on a trust walk? You are blindfolded while a friend leads you, perhaps through the woods or the city. You are left to be led just by their voice instructions to avoid a tree or a curb or a car. Or trust falls. Your friend stands behind you and asks you to fall back and they will catch you. We let ourselves fall back, trusting that our friend is really there and is able to catch us. Believe me, it is not easy. Is my friend trustworthy? Is she attentive enough and strong enough to catch me? It is a small example of what it means to trust a loving, heavenly Father with our whole lives.

Awakening Our Sleeping Child

Oue main concern here is entering that childlike joy that we once had, and that many of us have lost. It is the ability to trust, to play, to laugh, to love — for to such belongs the kingdom of heaven. We may need a resurrection of sorts, to wake up that childlike part of us that has gone dormant.

One great benefit in reading stories like those written by Tolkien or Lewis is that they can awaken that child within us. One of the attractions of these stories is the way they develop the idea of play. It is while the Pevensie children are playing hide-and-seek that Lucy discovers a magic wardrobe that leads her into the whole new world of Narnia. Tolkien portrays the Shire, where the hobbits live, as an idyllic, childlike place filled with eating and drinking, laughter and play, and the sharing of stories and the simple pleasures of life. Some would say Tolkien created his Middle Earth fantasy to escape the dull, dreary world of literary critics he had to endure on a daily basis. Yes, it may be true that these fantasies are an escape, but they are the kind of escape that can open our eyes to a greater reality. Both Lewis and Tolkien believed that the development of one's imagination is essential to grasping some of the deeper truths of life. We must move beyond pure logic and analysis to discover the most important gifts of life: love and laughter, trust and faith, and, of course, joy.

One of my longtime friends and colleagues is Jim Sire, PhD in English and for many years a senior editor at InterVarsity Press. For years we traveled together around Eastern Europe giving Christian apologetics–type teachings to university students. He is a great thinker, and we often engaged in weighty conversation, which I fully enjoyed. Jim also has what I would call a well-nurtured child in him. And frequently, at the most erudite moments of our discourse, he would get this twinkle in his eye. Something in our conversation struck him as funny. He is also a great punster. I would try to continue making what I thought was some profound point, but it was no use. He would start to smile, then snicker, then let out a full belly laugh. And I had no choice but to join in the fun and let him come out with what brought on this humored reaction. My times with Jim serve as a reminder to me that even in my greatest intellectual endeavors, I must make room for the child in me to come out.

How is your inner child doing? Is he still alive? Is she still able to lead you into some of your highest times of joy? Maybe it is time to unabashedly rediscover this playful side of you.

Reflection Questions

1. In contrasting the words *childish* and *childlike*, can you make a list of the differing characteristics that each word suggests?

2. What is it about children that moved Jesus to say, "Let the little children come to me and do not hinder them, for to such belongs the kingdom of heaven"?

3. Some people are able to look back on a generally happy childhood. For others, it was tragic, dark, and heavy. Maybe their childhood was cut short way too soon. Where do you find yourself on this spectrum? What factors or events contributed to this? Have you sought healing from this?

4. Many of us have gladly put our childhood behind us as we become adults. Is it hard for you to be childlike — carefree, trusting, even silly and fun-loving?

5. Do you feel that you have a joyful relationship with a loving heavenly Father, that you can trust him and rest in his loving arms? How might you recover this delightful way of living?

6

Friends of Joy

Susan was a missionary in Romania, very gifted and intelligent, a part of the international team working with university students. As coordinator for Eastern Europe, I was supervising this team and visiting them regularly. During one visit our team leader asked me to talk with Susan because she was not doing well. She was driving herself very hard — working constantly, not getting enough sleep — and her health was deteriorating. We were concerned that we might have to send Susan home to restore her health. So I talked with her. I said, "Susan, we are concerned about your health and overwork. You have said that you believe that God called you to Romania for life, but we may have to send you home. You are going to need to learn what it means to rest in Jesus, really rest." I shared the passage in Matthew 11:28–30, where Jesus invites us to come to him and find rest for our souls. She responded, "You're right. I am going to get up forty-five minutes earlier for the next three months to study everything the Bible has to say about rest." I just smiled. Finally she said, "That's probably not what you had in mind, is it?" "No," I said. But Susan did learn to rest in Jesus. Her health improved, and I am happy to report that she is still serving the Lord, joyfully, in Romania.

While I have tried to be clear that there is not a formula for success in finding joy, the Bible does point us to some "friends" of joy — God-given gifts, attitudes, and activities that will enrich and deepen our experience of joy. They may not be what you would expect. For example, the first one is Sabbath, the gift of rest.

Sabbath: The Gift of Rest

Let's begin with some pithy quotes from Rabbi Abraham Joshua Heschel:

> The greatest hope for the progress of mankind is the Sabbath.

> Shabbat comes with its own holiness; we enter not simply a day, but an atmosphere.

> Man is not a beast of burden, and the Sabbath is not for the purpose of enhancing the efficiency of his work.

> Labor is a craft; rest is an art.[1]

To be joyful, generally, we need to set aside special times to devote ourselves to joy. In the Hebrew Scriptures God's people are offered the gift of Sabbath rest. I realize that many people may not think of Sabbath as a gift, or even a positive experience at all. Nevertheless, Sabbath is a creation gift, and the term is first applied in relation to God himself. The Hebrew word *shabbat* simply means to cease, to stop. Sabbath was established as an ordinance for the benefit of humanity, to rescue us from slipping into a dull and meaningless existence. Imagine life without Sabbath rest — an endless, monotonous flow of days.

First, let's look at the origin of this creation gift of Sabbath:

> Thus the heavens and the earth were finished, and all the host of
> them. And on the seventh day God finished his work that he had
> done, and he rested on the seventh day from all his work that
> he had done. So God blessed the seventh day and made it holy,
> because on it God rested from all his work that he had done in
> creation. (Gen. 2:1–3)

The first two gifts God gave to humanity were work and rest.
And these are gifts that God himself exercises; he is portrayed as
the first worker and the first rester. Work is a wonderful gift that
provides dignity and meaning to our lives. Sabbath rest is equally
vital to living well, to flourishing. God has built this rhythm into
the universe. We can ignore it, but it will be to our peril. We will
suffer serious loss to our physical and emotional health, a loss of
what it means to be human and made in God's image. And we will
miss out on wonderful times of joy.

In the creation account, God takes time at the end of each day
to consider his work and to pronounce it good. We also need to
build time for work and rest into each day, each week. Time to reflect on who we are and who God is. To consider God's goodness in
our lives, and how he has spoken to us. What happened to us today?
How did we respond? Who did we encounter? What conversations
did we have? How was God present in those conversations?

Sabbath is more than just taking a day off work. It is a mindset,
a restful posture toward life. As Tim Keller states: "There's a work
underneath our work that we really need rest from. It's the work
of self-justification."[2]

If we are constantly trying to prove ourselves to other people or
to God, to make ourselves look good and to justify ourselves, then

we are never at rest, even when we look like we are. And this kind of work (proving ourselves) is the hardest work we will do, and the most unsatisfying, because it is never done, and it is never enough.

It is possible to bring Sabbath even into our daily work, when we learn to live in that restfulness that God brings to those who trust in him, rather than striving to continually make ourselves look better. We are invited to live in the experience of God's grace. It is grace that saves us, grace that keeps us, and grace that allows us to truly rest. Learning to bring rest into our Sabbath, and Sabbath into our work, is a key to joyful living.

In a way, life is like a river, always flowing. Each day there are more events, more conversations, some victories and some failures. It can feel at times like life is just passing us by. More things keep happening than we can keep track of. It is not a pleasant feeling. How do we stop the flow? How do we make sense of it all? We need Sabbath — to step out of the river, so to speak, and consider who we are and where this is all going. Socrates's famous statement in Plato's *Apology* is "The unexamined life is not worth living." There are many aspects of God's gift of the Sabbath, but one is that it provides space for us to step aside to reflect on our lives. I once took some Sabbath time to write a letter to my father, who had died a few years before. I never felt that I had come to closure with his passing. He died at age sixty-seven, much too soon for us. I poured out my heart to him in that letter, and for the first time I felt closure. I was grateful for his life and for the life he gave to me, and I felt that I was ready to move on. It was a "stepping out of the river" moment.

And so, we are given this weekly cycle: six days of work, one day of rest, further established by Moses in the law (Exod. 20:8). The gift of Sabbath began to be abused very early in biblical history. Many Israelites, greedy for more productivity and lacking trust in God's provision, began to let work crowd out the Sabbath. The prophets spoke out against these abuses continually. Amos reprimanded the people who were saying, "When will the new moon be over, that we may sell grain? And the Sabbath, that we may offer wheat for sale . . . ?" (Amos 8:5). When we come to the New Testament, we find the Pharisees abusing the Sabbath by turning it into a legalistic straitjacket, even condemning Jesus for healing on the Sabbath.

Today we see these same abuses. "Workaholism" keeps many in our culture from enjoying God's rest. Such people work nonstop, without days off or holidays, seeking to validate their existence by their work. Their whole identity is wrapped up in their work, and so work becomes an addiction. I have a friend in Japan who began a ministry with retired Japanese businessmen. When these men retire, it creates a crisis. Their whole life had been centered on their work and on socializing with coworkers. They usually left home before the family was awake and returned home after they were in bed, seven days a week. Their wives were often strangers and they had no relationship with their children. Retirement left a huge vacuum in their lives. The suicide rate is high among these retired businessmen. But my friend also found an openness to spiritual things among these men that had not been present earlier in their lives.

On the other side of the spectrum are those who, like the Pharisees, observe the Sabbath with regularity but impose on it a dreary legalism, such that fun and too much joy are frowned upon. It is no wonder that many children, growing up in legalistic homes where the practice of Sabbath was a drudgery, have turned away from the experience of Sabbath altogether.

But Jesus made it clear that "the Sabbath was made for man, not man for the Sabbath" (Mark 2:27). To listen to the Pharisees, one would think that God first made the Sabbath, then had to scramble to make human beings so that he would have someone to keep the Sabbath. But of course, it was the other way around. The minute

Sabbath gets turned into a burdensome chore, it ceases to be the gift that God intended for us.

But if we make the Sabbath our delight, we will find it to be a great source of joy in the Lord. This is the promise of Isaiah 58.

> "If you keep your feet from breaking the Sabbath
>   and from doing as you please on my holy day,
> *if you call the Sabbath a delight*
>   and the Lord's holy day honorable,
> and if you honor it by not going your own way
>   and not doing as you please or speaking idle words,
> *then you will find your joy in the Lord,*
>   and I will cause you to ride in triumph on
>   the heights of the land
>   and to feast on the inheritance of your
>   father Jacob."
> For the mouth of the LORD has spoken.
>
> (Isa. 58:13–14, emphasis mine)

In Sabbath rest, we show ourselves to be truly sons and daughters of a loving, heavenly Father who cares for us and provides for us. Sabbath reminds us of our humanness, our finiteness and dependence upon God. In observing times of rest, we allow ourselves the opportunity to look back on our labor (as God did) and give thanks for work well done. I often say at the end of a workday, "It's not perfect, but it's good." In Sabbath, we rest beneath God's smile and it brings us joy. It has been said that Sabbath is the great leveler of humanity. In Sabbath there are no employers and employees, no professionals and non-professionals, no teachers and pupils, just people, all made in God's image. In the Jewish law, everyone was to rest on the Sabbath — land-owners, slaves, aliens, even animals and the land (Deut. 5:12–15).

As we see in the Isaiah 58 passage, Sabbath is much more than just getting refueled to go back to work. It is not intended simply to increase our efficiency on the job. It is not like the Indy 500, where the cars zoom in for the pit stop, where they are refueled, jacked up, given new tires, and pushed back out into the race. Instead, Sabbath is an opportunity to rediscover our shalom, our peace and well-being, to restore our souls, to reflect on our lives. Where have we been, and where are we going? What is it that makes our life worth living? This is the full and abundant life Jesus intends for us. We are not just working machines, designed to keep producing on the treadmill of life. Jesus's invitation is "Come to me and find rest for your souls." We are invited to treat ourselves to daily and weekly times of restorative rest.

Do yourself a favor. Make the Sabbath your friend, your delight, and you will find joy in the Lord.

Gratitude: Cultivating a Grateful Heart

Thou that hast giv'n so much to me,
Give one thing more, a grateful heart

. . . .

Not thankful, when it pleaseth me;
As if thy blessings had spare days:
But such a heart whose pulse may be
Thy praise.[3]

I must confess how much these words penned by George Herbert resonate with me. I am so often an ungrateful person. I have stated earlier that I am not easily depressed, but I am not easily impressed either. I often take God's bountiful gifts for granted, so that I also cry out, "Lord, since you have given me so much, can you give me just one more thing? A grateful heart." Why is it so hard, when it seems so simple, to just be a thankful person? And why is my thankfulness so often short-lived and bland?

It is imperative that we come to the place of understanding that all of life is a gift — my breath, my mind, my body, and all the wonders of this marvelous creation. But it is so easy to slip into an attitude of entitlement, the idea that somehow, I deserve all these good things. We may find ourselves caught in the "What have you done for me lately, God?" frame of mind. The cup is always half empty. In this case, we will never be satisfied, we will never be truly thankful, and we will never be happy.

Many of us give thanks at meals, for God's provision of food, and this has taken on new meaning for me in recent years. I have begun to recite along with James, "Every good gift and every perfect gift is from above, coming down from the Father of lights, with whom there is no variation or shadow due to change" (James 1:17).

Paul makes perhaps the most far-reaching statement about giving thanks for God's good gifts. In contrast to the ascetic (self-denying) attitude that places restrictions on God's creation gifts, Paul condemns the false teaching of abstinence from marriage and food, strongly stating that all of God's creation is good. This flies in the face of the Greek notion that the material world is evil. Here is Paul's warning about the false teachers:

> They forbid people to marry and order them to abstain from certain foods, which God created to be received with thanksgiving by those who believe and who know the truth. For everything God created is good, and nothing is to be rejected if it is received with thanksgiving, because it is consecrated by the word of God and prayer. (1 Tim. 4:3–5)

Paul's world-affirming stance encourages believers to happily and thankfully enter into marriage and to eat all manner of food, which, he says, is consecrated (set apart as holy) by our prayer. This adds an important dimension to our meal-time prayers of thanks, which can often become quite rote and dull. Like Paul, we ought to consider eating as a sacred act!

A grateful spirit goes hand in hand with joy. Thankful people are joyful people. When we have a heart open to thanksgiving, we are also open to many other realities and perspectives, such as God's presence and graciousness toward us and our dependence on God for his provision. We become aware of how blessed we are and recognize the fullness of life Jesus offers. We see ourselves being held in the loving arms of the Almighty. We remember the goodness of God in our lives. (Some of us have known that goodness for a very long time.)

One of the saddest consequences of atheism and the secular mindset, in my view, is that there is really no one to thank. Of course, anyone can thank a person for a kindness done to them. But what about being deeply thankful for the gift of life, the beauty of the world, the wonder of music, and our ability to enjoy it all? If the world is simply a chance alignment of random circumstances, then there is no cause for being grateful for the beauty of a flower, the loveliness of a Bach sonata, or the orderliness of the changing seasons. And with that loss of gratefulness is a lost opportunity for joy.

We humans are a forgetful bunch, suffering from a sort of spiritual amnesia. We quickly grow indifferent to the blessings of life. Alexander Schmemann speaks of the great sin of failing to give thanks to God. We forget that in eating and breathing, we are continually receiving life from God.

In the recent movie *A Beautiful Day in the Neighborhood*, which is based on a true story, Fred Rogers (played by Tom Hanks) has an encounter with a reporter who is doing an article on him for

Esquire magazine. The reporter is cynical about life and skeptical about Rogers's TV show, having been hurt by his own father who has now come back into his life. Angry and unable to forgive his father, the reporter is frustrated and finds it hard to get time to interview Rogers. Finally, Rogers invites the reporter to lunch at his favorite restaurant. After some good conversation, Rogers asks the reporter if he would be willing to join him in a little one-minute exercise that he likes to practice: to just pause and be silent, and "be grateful for those who gave us life." Reluctantly, the reporter agrees. Then they begin the minute of silence, which seems like a long time on a movie screen. The camera scans the other tables in the restaurant, and slowly all the people at those tables stop their conversations and join the silent exercise of gratitude. Apparently, Mr. Rogers frequented this particular restaurant, and the people knew this exercise! We see Mr. Rogers's eyes tenderly viewing all the people as they become quiet. Then his eyes look directly into the camera, and I realized that this was an invitation for me, sitting in the theater, to take a moment to give thanks for those who gave me life. So I did, and it was good. And it made me feel very warm and joyful.

Who are the people who gave you life? Certainly your parents. But also others who have invested in you along the way, some who have spoken into your life — maybe a teacher, a mentor, a relative, a friend. There are several names that come immediately to my mind. Can I invite you, right now, to take one minute to express to God your gratitude for them? Maybe even write their names in a journal or on a card. I have found this to be a meaningful exercise along the way to joy.

It is so easy to forget, or to take for granted, the most essential gifts from God to us. When Moses spoke the words of the Shema (Hebrew for "Hear" or "Listen," the first word in the section) in Deuteronomy 6:4–8, he followed with a warning:

And when the LORD your God brings you into the land that he swore to your fathers, to Abraham, to Isaac, and to Jacob, to give you — with great and good cities that you did not build, and houses full of all good things that you did not fill, and cisterns that you did not dig, and vineyards and olive trees that you did not plant — and when you eat and are full, then *take care lest you forget* the LORD, who brought you out of the land of Egypt, out of the house of slavery. (Deut. 6:10–12, emphasis mine)

When, at the height of the British Empire, Rudyard Kipling wrote his poem "Recessional" for Queen Victoria's Diamond Jubilee, he punctuated it with a solemn refrain:

> Lord God of Hosts, be with us yet,
> Lest we forget — lest we forget!

The Hebrew festivals were times of celebration and great joy. They were also times of remembering. They were designed to help the people remember the Lord's goodness and faithfulness, his gracious working in history. Here is a description of the Festival of Tabernacles:

And you shall *rejoice* before the LORD your God at the place he will choose as a dwelling for his Name — you, your sons and daughters, your male and female servants, the Levites in your towns, and the foreigners, the fatherless and the widows living among you. *Remember* that you were slaves in Egypt and follow carefully these decrees.

Celebrate the Festival of Tabernacles for seven days after you have gathered the produce of your threshing floor and your winepress. *Be joyful at your festival* — you, your sons and daughters, your male and female servants, and the Levites, the foreigners, the fatherless and the widows who live in your towns. For seven days *celebrate* the festival to the LORD your God at the place the LORD will choose. For the LORD your God will *bless you* in all your harvest and in all the work of your hands, and *your joy will be complete*. (Deut. 16:11–15 NIV, emphasis mine)

The three great Old Testament festivals (Passover, Pentecost, Tabernacles) involved a pilgrimage to Jerusalem. They provided a rhythm to the year for the Israelites and, as I mentioned, a time of prescribed remembering:

- Remember that you were slaves in Egypt.
- Remember how I saved you and delivered you out of Egypt.
- Remember that you wandered forty years in the wilderness.
- Remember how I provided food and water for you in the wilderness.
- Remember the many harvests you enjoyed at my hand.

As the pilgrim caravans walked along the road up to Jerusalem, they sang their songs, the psalms of ascent (120–134). These included laughter and shouts of joy (126:2), as well as prayers for the city. They were aware of their deep dependence on God.

Some Christian traditions follow a liturgical calendar as a way of remembering God's redemptive work throughout the year. Christmas and Easter are the major feasts. Some of us have important family traditions surrounding these holidays. We take time to remember the Lord's supreme deliverance in the coming of Messiah. We remember Jesus's death and resurrection during Holy Week and Easter. These are the great redemptive movements of God in history.

Chapter 6

I have many wonderful memories of our children and grandchildren coming home for the Christmas holiday, sometimes camping out in our house for five to seven days. When this happens, it feels like a festival, perhaps similar to the ancient Hebrew festivals. There is a certain timelessness about it. There is good conversation around good food, and music — lots of music.

Yet I often come away, from the Christmas celebration especially, wondering, What happened? Where did it go? I had such grand intentions that this year we would make Christmas special. We would get caught up in the drama and the wonder of the story of Christ's coming as a child, the greatest gift. To be sure, we enjoyed a measure of this wonderful truth, but in many ways it seemed to slip away, again.

It seems such a simple thing, to be grateful people. Author Mike Mason suggests that we should adopt a simple practice: start each day by giving thanks for five things that are true for us, through which we experience God's goodness.[4] I have tried this with some measure of success — as I roll out of bed, to give thanks — though morning may not be my best time. Even when I have not slept well and do not feel very rested, I can express that to God, and then move on to things that I am nevertheless thankful for.

As I walk my neighborhood, give thanks at mealtimes, or respond to deep readings of Scripture — these are my best experiences of gratefulness. I find myself saying, "Lord, your garden is still flourishing and beautiful on the earth." "Lord, your wisdom is so amazing." I have sometimes looked up into a starry night sky, lifted my hands up in amazement, sometimes even clapped my hands, and rather than think of how small and insignificant I am, I shout, "Wow, my Father made all that." It is sheer joy.

Giving thanks, even when we don't feel like it, eventually produces a life of gratitude, which engenders a life of joy, which brings glory to God.

Full Repentance: A Cleansed Conscience

It should not have come as a surprise to me that there are repeated references to joy in the psalms of repentance. And yet I was startled when I first saw this connection. This spiritual discipline, the exercise of full repentance, restores our joy.

It is no mystery that the works of the flesh are continually at work in us, and they always steal our joy. Consider again this list of joy thieves:

Sexual immorality, impurity and debauchery; idolatry and witchcraft; hatred, discord, jealousy, fits of rage, selfish ambition, dissensions, factions and envy; drunkenness, orgies, and the like. (Gal. 5:19–21)

Some of these may bring temporary pleasure and comfort, but never joy. We cannot be joyful and hate at the same time. We cannot feel jealousy and simultaneously experience joy. Indulging in lust and sexual fantasy may offer gratification, but it will rob us of our joy every time.

What then? Since we so frequently give way to sinful thoughts and feelings — and even the greatest people of faith in the Bible, like David, fell into sin — how do we restore our joy?

The answer is, of course, repentance. But not the timid, half-hearted repentance that we so often mistake for the real thing. *Full* repentance, *true* repentance, will ultimately lead to restored joy.

Consider David's great psalm of repentance, Psalm 51:

Purge me with hyssop, and I shall be clean;
    wash me, and I shall be whiter than snow.
Let me hear joy and gladness;
    let the bones that you have broken rejoice.

Hide your face from my sins,
    and blot out all my iniquities.
Create in me a clean heart, O God,
    and renew a right spirit within me.
Cast me not away from your presence,
    and take not your Holy Spirit from me.
Restore to me the *joy* of your salvation,
    and uphold me with a willing spirit.

                    (Ps. 51:7–12, emphasis mine)

For a long time, I assumed that the way I would know I had successfully repented of sin was by the level of remorse I felt. Indeed, this is an important part of repentance. To be genuinely sorry for my sin, to be broken over my moral failures, to come to an understanding of the seriousness of my selfish words and behavior is essential to authentic repentance. I know this is a step of true repentance, but it is not the end of repentance.

I also knew that repentance meant doing an about-face with regard to my sin. I need to turn around 180 degrees. I need to honestly desire, by God's grace, to change, to move in a new direction. I know that I can be far too easy on myself. I tend to excuse my own selfish attitudes and actions while at the same time judging others for similar ones. Biblical repentance does require a change of attitude, thinking, and behavior. But this is not the end of repentance.

As I reflected again on Psalms 32 and 51, as I often do when I need repentance in my life, I noticed a new sign of repentance. Full repentance leads to restored joy. At first, this caught me by surprise. I had never thought of repentance and joy together. And yet it is clear that David viewed restored joy as the fruit of repentance.

The problem with our repentance, with *my* repentance, is that it often stops short. It is truncated. We may have sincere sorrow for our sins, we may earnestly confess our transgressions, we may have a heartfelt desire to turn away from our sin. But the END of repentance is supposed to be "joy and gladness." We are often heavy on remorse and light on the joy of forgiveness. Even after his sin with Bathsheba, David boldly asks God to "restore to me the joy of your salvation." To "let the bones you have broken rejoice." Confession and repentance should leave us not sad and sorrowful but with a deep sense of forgiveness and cleansing, redirected toward God to love and to serve him, and full of joy and a sense of relief.

True repentance will turn our "mourning into dancing" (Ps. 30:11–12):

> You have turned for me my mourning into dancing;
>   you have loosed my sackcloth
>   and clothed me with gladness,
> that my glory may sing your praise and not be silent.
>   O Lord my God, I will give thanks to you forever!

The image that comes to my mind as I reflect on these words is from the film *The Mission*. Robert De Niro plays Rodrigo Mendoza, an eighteenth-century Portuguese mercenary who is murdering and enslaving the Native peoples of South America. After murdering his own brother in a jealous rage, he is filled with remorse and is utterly hopeless. Then a Jesuit priest begins to minister to him. Because Mendoza is a man of action, the priest gives him a task of penance: he must climb a steep cliff while carrying his instruments of violence (swords, shields, guns) in a sack on his back. When he finally reaches the top of the cliff, the leader of the Guarani community, whose members he has been killing, approaches him with a knife and, after a tense moment, rather than killing him, cuts the ropes off his sack. As Mendoza watches all his former weapons go tumbling down the cliff and realizes that this Native convert to Christian faith has cut him free from this burden, he begins to weep with great sobs and flowing tears. As the camera closes in on De Niro's face, we see his weeping continue, until finally it begins slowly to change to tears of laughter and release and great joy. What a picture of repentance and restoration!

We may not know whether this quote attributed to Martin Luther — "Sin boldly and repent more boldly still" — is authentic. And we may question the wisdom of advising people to sin boldly. But the admonishment to "repent more boldly still" is right on target.

As joyous as Mendoza felt after being relieved of his burden, how much more can we rejoice that once for all, Jesus has taken our sins upon himself in his atoning work on the cross. And with it, he takes on himself our suffering, misery, unhappiness, bitterness, and disappointment, that we might be free to know this amazing joy.

The writer of Hebrews speaks of the wonderful gift of a *cleansed conscience.*

> Therefore, brothers, since we have confidence to enter the holy places by the blood of Jesus, by the new and living way that he opened for us through the curtain, that is, through his flesh, and since we have a great priest over the house of God, let us draw near with a true heart in full assurance of faith, with our hearts sprinkled clean from an evil conscience and our bodies washed with pure water. (Heb. 10:19–22)

Counselors and therapists can assist us in dealing with guilt, whether imagined or real. But it is only the blood of Jesus that can provide us with a cleansed conscience. This is a promise we can claim. This is the kind of confident, complete, full assurance God intends for us and wants for us. But we so often stop short and miss out on the full blessing of a cleansed conscience. We sing of the "grace that is greater than all our sin," but do we believe it, and can we step into this all-encompassing grace? Do you have a sin so great that even God cannot forgive the terrible offense, such that even the blood of Jesus is not sufficient? Is your sin greater than murder and adultery? These were David's sins, and he was washed clean, forgiven, and restored to joy.

Think of the people to whom Jesus offered forgiveness. There is the woman, a prostitute, who washed his feet with her tears, who was "forgiven much" (Luke 7:36–50). Jesus says to her, "Your faith has saved you; go in peace." There was the paralyzed man who was healed *and* forgiven. And Zacchaeus the tax collector, who was set free from his self-made prison of ill-gotten wealth. Mary Magdalene was set free from seven evil spirits; Jesus had given her back her life. There is the Samaritan woman at the well who received living water and found her Messiah.

So the next time we employ David's great psalm of repentance, Psalm 51, as a means of expressing our own confession and repentance, let's follow it through to its conclusion. Let our mourning be turned into dancing, let our crushed bones rejoice, so that we may step into the great gift of restored joy. This is what God has for us. This is what God wants for us. Isn't this what we long for — to be free from the burden of guilt? Joy has a voice. It is the voice of Jesus saying, "Go in peace," "Your sins are forgiven," "Neither do I condemn you," "Come to me and find rest."

Let us also do that priestly work with one another, offering grace and forgiveness to one another. Sometimes we need someone to say to us, "Dear brother/sister, I have seen your repentance. Please know that your sins are forgiven. Please accept God's gift of a cleansed conscience. By the authority of Christ, and his blood shed for you, I tell you that you are cleansed, washed, forgiven, set free. Believe it, know it, and step into this new life."

Let us boldly step into the joy that God intends for us. And to know that joy, we need to (1) make friends with the gift of Sabbath rest, (2) follow the path of gratitude, and (3) enter into the joy of full repentance.

Reflection Questions

1. How is your Sabbath rest? Do you have a practice of setting aside times for restoration, reflection, and renewal? What steps might you take to begin afresh?

2. Are you a grateful person, regularly thankful for God's continual good gifts? Would you be willing to take one simple step of thanking God for five things each morning?

3. Just as one of the joy-stealers is the sin and selfishness that creeps into our lives, one of the friends of joy is full repentance of sin. We have the promise of restored joy that comes with genuine repentance (Ps. 51:12). Have you discovered this joy?

4. Many of us suffer from shame and a guilty conscience. A cleansed conscience is a wonderful gift (Heb. 10:22). Have you discovered the freedom that comes from having a guilty conscience washed clean? Do you need to seek the help of a mature Christian counselor to help you through this process?

7

Enemies of Joy

Near the beginning of Tolkien's *Lord of the Rings* trilogy, Gandalf the wizard explains to Frodo the hobbit the foreboding darkness and the coming war against the evil Lord Sauron's forces that were overtaking Middle Earth. Frodo regrets having to live in this hard time, and what it will mean for him. No doubt many living in England during World War II had similar feelings as Hitler's armies were marching across Europe. Tolkien, like Lewis, lived through two world wars, and I am sure he knew the feeling of wishing at times that he had lived in another period of history. Some of us who have lived through the coronavirus lockdown may have had similar feelings.

> "I wish it need not have happened in my time," said Frodo.
> "So do I," said Gandalf, "and so do all who live to see such times. But that is not for them to decide. All we have to decide is what to do with the time that is given us."[1]

Jesus also lived on earth during a dark time when many evil forces were active. As Lewis describes, Jesus came into enemy-occupied territory. We can find joy in following in Jesus's footsteps, walking his path of love in the sacrificial giving of ourselves to others. There is joy in living under his gentle yoke, living a purposeful, productive, and restful life.

But what happens if we have lost the joy? I have been there. I mentioned earlier that my eldest daughter said to me one day, "Dad, you seem to have lost some of your joy lately." It was an understatement. And it was a gentle reminder that I needed to rethink my path. If our lives are characterized by gloom and toil, I think we have to conclude that it is no longer Jesus we are following. Somewhere along the way, we got offtrack. We have taken a serious detour.

Remember that Jesus is the source of authentic joy. It is his joy that he gives to us. If we pursue joy for its own sake, it will elude us. We might find ourselves more miserable than ever. But if we pursue the Joy-Giver himself and open our hearts to him and his joy, we can't miss it.

Joy has a voice. A big part of our spiritual struggle is distinguishing the voices that call out to us in our world — voices of success, voices of temptation, voices of accusation and condemnation (Rev. 12:10). Jesus said, "My sheep hear my voice, and I know them, and they follow me" (John 10:27). And again he says, "The sheep hear [the Shepherd's] voice, and he calls his own sheep by name and leads them out" (John 10:3). We need to train our ears to recognize God's voice — the one who made us, the one who has redeemed us, the one who loves us and wants the best for us. We need the Shepherd to lead us and to care for us. On one occasion Jesus looked at the crowds "and he had compassion on them, because they were harassed and helpless, like sheep without a shepherd" (Matt. 9:36).

When I find myself having lost my joy, I have also lost God's voice, the voice of the Shepherd. I have lost that sweet communion with him that comes from devoting myself to prayer and meditation on Scripture. It may sound simplistic, but feeding on God's word, the bread of life, has always been essential to me for staying on the path that leads to joy. When I wander from this source of nourishment, I begin to sense a dullness, a lostness, an anxiety settling into my mind, and my outlook on life turns bleak. I find myself trying to go it alone and failing. And in that failure, I am burdened down by guilt, and the joy is gone. I have lost my compass, my perspective.

So what are those "enemies of joy" that would get us off course, get us moving down a wrong path, and listening to another voice? What are the joy deflaters?

Despair and Sloth

The opposite of joy is not sadness or suffering, trouble or hardship. The opposite of joy is despair and hopelessness. It is this spirit that is behind Peter's threefold denial of the Lord. When we slip into despair, we are completely devoid of joy. To be without hope is misery. It is pure doom and gloom. The psalmist, Job, the Preacher in Ecclesiastes — all at times tasted the bitter cup of despair. Paul speaks of being "hard pressed on every side, but not crushed; perplexed, but not in despair" (2 Cor. 4:8). It is a mindset we must resist, by God's grace.

Life is a struggle. As the character Wesley says in the movie *The Princess Bride*, "Life is pain, Princess. Anyone who says different is selling something." Or, as psychiatrist M. Scott Peck says in his opening words of his book *The Road Less Traveled*, "Life is difficult"; the sooner we accept that fact, the healthier we will be.[2] The acceptance of genuine pain in our lives is one of the keys to mental and spiritual health. And as the apostle Paul said, "We do not wrestle against flesh and blood, but against the rulers, against the authorities, against the cosmic powers over this present darkness, against the spiritual forces of evil in the heavenly places" (Eph. 6:12). We are in a battle. This is war. Life is full of disappointment, frustration, disillusionment, temptation, and confusion. How we respond to this reality makes all the difference.

We are all tempted at times to give up the battle. It is only natural, because we were made for, and are destined for, joy and peace. But we live in this interlude where there is rampant evil and fierce struggle, which is not normal and is not the permanent state of affairs. Look back again at the opening to this chapter, the conversation between Frodo and Gandalf. When it comes to the battle, sometimes we would just like to sit this one out. To stay in this battle takes courage. It takes stamina and resilience. It is also natural that we will sometimes feel angry about the broken condition of our world and our own lives. And that anger can be converted into determination and passion to continue the fight.

The problem is that we are sorely tempted to avoid pain and struggle. We all feel weary and overwhelmed at times. But some respond by dropping out of the battle, having fallen into despair, complacency, resignation, even cynicism. They feel it has all just become too much, too hard. It's just not worth it. Many have given up, lacking the vision or courage to go on. They are sidelined from the battle, as a casualty. One of the greatest strategies of the Enemy is to take us out of the battle. He knows a secret about us: we hate to fight; we prefer comfort.

The classical word for this is "sloth," one of the seven deadly sins. We often associate sloth with laziness, but there is a greater danger than mere physical laziness, and that is mental or spiritual laziness. That's what the spiritual masters called sloth, or *acedia*.[3]

In her book *The Other Six Deadly Sins*, Dorothy Sayers presents a profoundly disturbing description of the sin of sloth. At its most extreme, it leads to a withdrawal from others, a loss of interest in life itself. Here is her description:

> The sixth deadly sin is named by the Church *acedia* or *sloth*. In the world it calls itself tolerance; but in hell it is called despair. It is the accomplice of the other sins and their worst punishment. It is the sin which believes in nothing, cares for nothing, seeks to know nothing, interferes with nothing, enjoys nothing, loves nothing, hates nothing, finds purpose in nothing, lives for nothing, and only remains alive because there is nothing it would die for.[4]

Those who are slothful may still be busy with activity, but they are dead inside; their heart is dead. All of life seems empty, without purpose or meaning. It is not hard to see that this state of living is utter joylessness and cheerlessness, and we can see why this is such a devastating enemy of joy.

When the battle seems to be hopeless and pointless, we may be tempted to despair, to give up and drop out. This world can be a dark and menacing place. We need to be comforted again by Jesus's words, "In the world you will have tribulation. But take heart; I have overcome the world" (John 16:33). We do know how this is all going to end! In fact, the battle has already been won. Why would we give up when we are on the winning side? Remember the apostle Paul's encouraging words: "And let us not grow weary of doing good, for in due season we will reap, if we do not give up. So then, as we have opportunity, let us do good to everyone, and especially to those who are of the household of faith" (Gal. 6:9–10).

Let me take a moment to make clear that I recognize that some people struggle with clinical depression, and I don't want to suggest that they are simply lazy or slothful for feeling emotionally empty and lacking energy. They may need to seek professional help, including medication to deal with the chemical imbalance.

Life can be a severe struggle at times. In this world of ours, one of the requisites of joy is learning to embrace the struggle.[5] I realize that many people dislike this "battle" terminology for the Christian life, and I acknowledge that it has sometimes been abused, with militant visions of conquest and crusades. But to be sure, this battle is like no other. It is not against flesh and blood, as Paul says, but against "cosmic powers," against "spiritual forces of evil" (Eph. 6:12). If we avoid the struggle, we will find ourselves sidelined in this grand work of God's kingdom, and we will surely lose our joy. "Rejoice in hope, be patient in tribulation, be constant in prayer" (Rom. 12:12).

Let's look at some examples of courage versus cowardice, or perseverance versus shrinking from the battle.

In *The Lord of the Rings* during the final battle for Gondor, the steward king, Denethor, has lost all hope. He had come to believe that it was futile to fight against Mordor, and that the sooner they gave up, the better off they would be. So we see him pining in his fortress, passive, dour, hopeless. Meanwhile, outside, the battle is raging, and the defenders of Gondor are fighting fiercely. But, as Peter Jackson so poignantly portrays it in the film version, they are fighting with excitement and hope, faces alight, excited to be in the battle, while Denethor only has a scowl. His is the face of joylessness.

Contrast this with Jesus, "who for the joy that was set before him endured the cross, despising the shame, and is seated at the right hand of the throne of God" (Heb. 12:2).

We see another example of sloth and cowardice in the life of Saul. When David came upon that famous scene with Israel and the Philistines encamped against each other, Goliath was mocking the Israelites and their God (1 Sam. 17). Saul was hiding in his tent, away from the battle, and it is "little David" who goes out and faces the enemy, without armor or sword but with the conviction that there is a God in Israel and that he would deliver the enemy into their hands.

On another occasion, Saul and the Israelite army are outnumbered and out-weaponed by the Philistines (Saul and Jonathan had the only two swords in the Israelite army!). Again, Saul remains passive while Jonathan takes his armor-bearer and, climbing a steep cliff, surprises a whole Philistine detachment, routs them, and sends the entire Philistine army fleeing in panic (1 Sam. 14). When Saul finally realizes what is happening, he comes to his senses and orders his army to chase after the fleeing Philistines.

These examples refer to actual physical battles, but I cite them to illustrate the difference between cowardice and courage. There is also metaphoric battle language used in the Scriptures that speaks of the battle in which we are all engaged:

> This charge I entrust to you, Timothy, my child, in accordance with the prophecies previously made about you, that by them you may wage the good warfare, holding faith and a good conscience. (1 Tim. 1:18–19)

> Fight the good fight of faith. (1 Tim. 6:12)

> Put on the whole armor of God, that you may be able to stand against the schemes of the devil. For we do not wrestle against flesh and blood, but against the rulers, against the authorities, against the cosmic powers over this present darkness, against the spiritual forces of evil in the heavenly places. (Eph. 6:11–12)

> Resist the devil and he will flee from you. (James 4:7)

In your struggle against sin you have not yet resisted to the point
of shedding your blood. (Heb. 12:4)

Jesus was gentle and loving with those in need, with the weak
and powerless. But we see another side of Jesus in his interactions
with the religious rulers (Matt. 23) and in his confrontation with
demonic spirits. He knew he was in "enemy-occupied territory." He
laid down his own life willingly, but he fought resolutely against
evil, hypocrisy, and self-righteousness.

You may have heard the story about the conversation between
the astrophysicist and the old preacher. The astrophysicist said, "You
know, when I think of Jesus, I like to think of the old children's prayer
'Gentle Jesus, Meek and Mild.'" The old preacher replied, "Yes, and
when I think of astrophysics, I like to think of 'Twinkle, Twinkle,
Little Star.'" In other words, to see Jesus as *only* "meek and mild" is
too simplistic. Jesus is gentle, compassionate, and loving, yes, but he
is also resolute, courageous, and filled with conviction.

In this battle, we need to be especially attentive in looking out
for one another. We all are tempted at times to give up. Some may
have lost heart, some may be battle-weary, some may have fallen —
and these are desperately in need of encouragement. The word "en-
courage" literally means to build courage into someone, and this is
a ministry we need to have in order to remain in the battle. This is
not a battle that we can or should try to fight alone. We are in this
together. At times we must call out for help, and at other times be
ready to offer help to others who are wounded.

The writer of Hebrews creates a picture of soldiers marching
along the line of battle in support of one another:

Therefore, strengthen the hands that are weak and the knees
that are feeble, and make straight paths for your feet, so that

the limb which is lame may not be put out of joint, but rather be healed. (Heb. 12:12–13 NASB)

Again, the Hebrews author enjoins us to take up the ministry of encouragement:

And let us consider how to stir up one another to love and good works, not neglecting to meet together, as is the habit of some, but encouraging one another, and all the more as you see the Day drawing near. (Heb. 10:23–24)

Fear and Worry

We have already briefly looked at this issue, but it is so essential to the life of joy that we must look at it more deeply. We are pitiful creatures. When we are joyless, we long for an experience of greater joy. But when we are feeling joyful and things are going quite well, we immediately begin to fret that we will lose our joy or the things that contribute to it. It might be our money, our investments, our job, our health, our family. Mike Mason says it well: "The quickest way to send your joy packing is to become afraid that it will leave or that something will happen to take it away. What a pitiful way to live! Nothing can be deeply enjoyed for fear it will soon be gone."[6] As Corrie Ten Boom reminds us, "Worrying is carrying tomorrow's load with today's strength — carrying two days at once. It is moving into tomorrow ahead of time. Worrying doesn't empty tomorrow of its sorrow, it empties today of its strength."[7]

In the movie *Joe Versus the Volcano*, I came across some profound theology. Joe (Tom Hanks) and his fellow traveler, Patricia (Meg Ryan), travel to a remote island in the Pacific plagued by an angry volcano, and a tribal chief is eager to offer them as a sacrifice to appease the volcano. He throws them into the volcano, but they are spewed out and land in the ocean. Whenever they survive some harrowing ordeal (like the volcano), Patricia points out how fortunate they are, but Joe says, "Well, yes, but . . ." And Patricia responds, "It's always going to be something with you, isn't it, Joe?" Doesn't that capture what is often our approach to life? Are we always going to find fault with our present circumstances, even when we have been rescued again and again?

Of the hundreds of people Brené Brown interviewed for her book *Daring Greatly*, 80 percent admitted to regularly letting their minds rehearse all the worst-case scenarios that might happen in their lives.[8] We see these scenarios in the news every day. We imagine getting the call from the police about a terrible accident. Getting the report from the doctor that the results showed cancer. We foolishly think we can guard ourselves against calamity by carefully imagining potential catastrophes and how we might control them or at least prepare ourselves for them. Knowing our tendency to do this, Jesus taught, "And which of you by being anxious can add a single hour to his span of life? . . . Therefore do not be anxious about tomorrow, for tomorrow will be anxious for itself. Sufficient for the day is its own trouble" (Matt. 6:27, 34).

This "foreboding joy," as Brown calls it, comes to us when things are going well. And so we rob ourselves of enjoying the moment by worrying about how it will all end. In trying to avoid the pain and disappointment of loss, we sacrifice the genuine experience of joy. "Perhaps you have stood over your children while they are sleeping, they look so peaceful and angelic, and your heart swells with joy and love and gratitude."[9] But then the dread creeps in and joy fades and disappears. We don't want to be blindsided. We don't want to be caught off guard. We don't want to admit how vulnerable we are, and how dependent we are on God's sovereign grace. Yes, life is fragile. We are mortal, and we are vulnerable to all manner of disappointment and loss. But if we are unwilling to accept and live with this reality, if we are unwilling to entrust ourselves to God's care, it will continually destroy our joy.

I found myself doing this during one of our family Christmas gatherings. It was a wonderful time of sharing food, stories, struggles, lively dinner conversations, music, games, and more music. We were to be together for five days, camping out in our house with our whole family. But very soon into the gathering, I began to lament that it would all soon come to an end. I began to feel gloomy. Finally, I shook myself and said, "Hey, this is robbing you of your joy. It is keeping you from enjoying the moment." It worked. But still, on and off during that week, the gloom would return. This is no doubt partly explained by the fact that we have eternity written in our hearts (Eccles. 3:11). We long for timelessness. This is how God made us. But it is more likely the result of my lack of faith, my unwillingness to accept limitations, and my inability to fully trust God with my life.

Brené Brown suggests that most of us live in fear because we are afraid of being "found out." We are afraid of being vulnerable and honest with people, of showing our weakness, and so we live to constantly avoid shame. We want to make ourselves look good, competent, and strong, but none of us is invincible, so we live in fear. Have you ever had nightmares where you forget to put on some of your clothes or you find yourself naked in a public setting? For me, I am preaching, or teaching a class, but I forgot my pants and am hiding behind the podium hoping people won't notice. Well, that is the fear of shaming that we live with.

Biblically, we understand this condition to have its origin in the fallen state of humanity. An aspect of that "foul revolt" of which Milton speaks in *Paradise Lost* is a refusal to accept our creaturely limitations and our predisposition to control instead of trust. The Lord is God, and we are not. The Lord is all-powerful and all-knowing, and we are not. We can resonate with the Enemy's tactic: "Did God really say, 'You must not eat from any tree in the garden'?" (Gen. 3:1). This is the insinuation that follows: Is God holding out on you? Why would God place these limitations on you?

This is all compounded by our self-serving bias, our pride, and our arrogant posture toward other people and God's creation, as well as by our unwillingness to trust God to care for us. Surely the antidote to worry is to trust in a loving, heavenly Father who cares for us, and to practice gratitude for the good gifts he does bring into our lives.

Much of the "futility" described in the book of Ecclesiastes is a result of this unwillingness to accept our human limitations. Peter Leithart points out that "some have read Ecclesiastes as the bitter reflections of an aging impotent cynic; others have read it as a hedonistic tract — Eat, drink, and be merry. Solomon regularly punctuates his meditations with exhortations to enjoy life: 'there is nothing better for a man than to eat and drink and tell himself that his labor is good' (Eccles. 2:24–25)."[10] But this is not the main message of Ecclesiastes. It is a call to accept life as a gift from God, and to live a life of faith in spite of our limited ability to control our own destiny or to unravel all the mysteries of life. We may not be able to figure out all of life's riddles, but if we can accept our common human situation, our finiteness, as God's good gift to us, we can find "gladness of heart" (Eccles. 5:18–20).

The command to "fear not," or "do not be afraid," is repeated hundreds of times in the Bible. In Isaiah, God reminds the people, "Fear not, for I am with you; be not dismayed, for I am your God; I will strengthen you, I will help you, I will uphold you with my righteous right hand" (Isa. 41:10).

Jesus reminds his disciples, "Are not two sparrows sold for a penny? And not one of them will fall to the ground apart from your Father. But even the hairs of your head are all numbered. Fear not, therefore; you are of more value than many sparrows" (Matt. 10:29–31). These verses should be a regular part of our arsenal in our struggle against fear and worry. As Bob Dylan states it in his song "Every Grain of Sand": "Then onward in my journey I come to understand / that every hair is numbered, like every grain of sand."

Let's look again at Jesus's teaching in the Sermon on the Mount, where he directly confronts this tendency toward fear and worry and anxiety.

> "Therefore I tell you, do not be anxious about your life, what you will eat or what you will drink, nor about your body, what you will put on. Is not life more than food, and the body more than clothing? Look at the birds of the air: they neither sow nor reap nor gather into barns, and yet your heavenly Father feeds them. Are you not of more value than they? And which of you by being anxious can add a single hour to his span of life? And why are you anxious about clothing? Consider the lilies of the field, how they grow: they neither toil nor spin, yet I tell you, even Solomon in all his glory was not arrayed like one of these. But if God so clothes the grass of the field, which today is alive and tomorrow is thrown into the oven, will he not much more clothe you, O you of little faith? Therefore do not be anxious, saying, 'What shall we eat?' or 'What shall we drink?' or 'What shall we wear?' For the Gentiles seek after all these things, and your heavenly Father knows that you need them all. But seek first the kingdom of God and his righteousness, and all these things will be added to you.

"Therefore do not be anxious about tomorrow, for tomorrow will be anxious for itself. Sufficient for the day is its own trouble." (Matt. 6:25–34)

J. I. Packer was speaking to a group of InterVarsity staff at a conference on the Sermon on the Mount. One staff member asked him, "Dr. Packer, where is *grace* in the Sermon on the Mount? It seems so heavy and demanding." Packer replied, "It is in that important, repeating word — *Father*. Your Father knows that you need these things and he cares for you." Indeed, this passage is full of grace, and the invitation is to trust our Father to care for us rather than to worry about all these things. Imagine what it would be like to live without worry! And this is exactly how Jesus wants his disciples to live.

In response to our preoccupation with worry and anxiety, Jesus uses gentle reassurance. He appeals to everyday images: the birds of the air, the flowers of the field. As Luther says, Jesus "is making the birds our schoolmasters and teachers. It is a great and abiding disgrace to us that in the Gospel a helpless sparrow should become a theologian and a preacher to the wisest of men."[11] Charles Spurgeon says, "Lovely lilies, how ye rebuke our foolish nervousness!"[12] And John Stott cites this anonymous little poem:

> Said the robin to the sparrow
> I should really like to know
> Why these anxious human beings
> Rush about and hurry so.
> Said the sparrow to the robin,
> Friend, I think that it must be
> That they have no heavenly Father
> Such as cares for you and me.

Jesus raises some fundamental questions in this Sermon. What do you treasure? How is your vision? Who do you serve? What do you seek most in life? These questions get at the core of our propensity to worry and fret. And to get our thinking straight about these central values will put us on the road to less anxiety and more joy.

There are three good reasons why we should not worry:

1. It is unproductive. What a waste of time and energy to worry and fret. It cannot add a single day to our lives.
2. It is unnecessary. You have a Father who knows you need these things. He wants your best, and he is looking out for you.
3. It is unworthy. This is the way the pagans live; it is not the way of life of those who would call themselves disciples of Jesus, those who have a loving Father who is all-powerful and all-knowing, and who cares for us.

At this point we may be feeling like Joe from *Joe Versus the Volcano*. We may say, "Yes, but what about . . . you know . . . the sparrow *does* fall." We do need to ask what is promised here, and what is not. Jesus is not promising that we will be protected against every calamity, every adversity. The sparrow does fall, but not without the Father's notice. He knows, he permits. Nothing is outside of his care and providence. The days of our life are ordained for us (Ps. 90). We are not promised exemption from trouble, hardship, sickness, persecution, loss, or death. It is all in God's good timing and purpose, and beyond our control. So what *is* the promise? It's that not one thing will happen apart from God's loving care and provision for us. Can we live with that? Is that enough? Can we trust God with that? Do we really have any other choice?

Chapter 7

Lord, help our lack of courage, our poor vision, our weak faith, our inability to trust, our feeble desires, and our tendency to settle for so little, when you have a lifetime of joy planned for us.

The Heavy Burden of Legalism

Falling into a legalistic mindset will swiftly steal our joy. It is one of the great enemies of joy. Paul's admonition to the Galatians is clear:

O foolish Galatians! Who has bewitched you? (Gal. 3:1)

Are you so foolish? Having begun by the Spirit, are you now being perfected by the flesh? (Gal. 3:3)

What then has become of your blessedness [i.e., joy]? (Gal. 4:15)

For freedom Christ has set us free; stand firm therefore, and do not submit again to a yoke of slavery. (Gal. 5:1)

Are you a "rules" person? Do you find yourself saying, "Just tell me what is expected of me and I will do it. I don't like vagueness." This can be a valuable quality. But it can also leave us as prey to the lure of legalism.

Paul wants to know: Who has stolen your joy? (Gal. 4:15). Why would you want to submit yourselves to following these heavy man-made rules about special days and circumcision, enslaving yourselves to your futile efforts in keeping the law? But there is always an attraction to this legalistic version of Christian faith — it is clear, simple, and comfortable. And above all, it seems doable. It appeals to our pride, and with pride comes self-exalting religion, and with that comes the end of joy. Joy is found when we exult in what God has done for us.

Jesus was continually battling against this legalistic mentality with the scribes and the Pharisees. Jesus's strongest, harshest words were against them, particularly this burden of legalism they insisted on placing on their own disciples.

"They tie up heavy burdens, hard to bear, and lay them on people's shoulders, but they themselves are not willing to move them with their finger." (Matt. 23:4)

"Woe to you, scribes and Pharisees, hypocrites! For you travel across sea and land to make a single proselyte, and when he becomes a proselyte, you make him twice as much a child of hell as yourselves." (Matt. 23:15)

Legalism inevitably leads to a showy form of religious expression and to hypocrisy. It is an externalized form of religion that seemed to creep into Jewish piety especially during the Babylonian exile and following. Jesus exposes the religious leaders for this hypocrisy:

"They do all their deeds to be seen by others. For they make their phylacteries broad and their fringes long, and they love the place of honor at feasts and the best seats in the synagogues and greetings in the marketplaces and being called rabbi by others." (Matt. 23:5–7)

"Woe to you, scribes and Pharisees, hypocrites! For you clean the outside of the cup and the plate, but inside they are full of greed and self-indulgence. You blind Pharisee! First clean the in-

side of the cup and the plate, that the outside also may be clean."
(Matt. 23:25–26)

This kind of religiosity involves trying to make yourself look good before others. A hypocrite is essentially a pretender. The word derives from ancient Greek theater, where the actors wore a mask. Later it took on the idea of wearing a figurative mask. It is fine to play a role onstage, but if we are acting in real life, then we have a problem. There is much confusion in popular culture about this term. A hypocrite is not someone who fails to live up to their own standards, for none of us, if we are honest, lives up to our own standards. A hypocrite is someone who pretends to be virtuous before others, but in reality, they fall far short.

A distinguishing mark of a Christian should be that we are able to admit our weakness, our faults, the fact that we sin against God and other people. Becky Manley Pippert tells the story of her college roommate who was not a believer. Becky was always trying to witness to her, but she felt like she was continually messing up and ruining her testimony. One day she decided to apologize to her roommate for being such a failure as a Christian. Her roommate said, "But that is what has impressed me about you, Becky: you are always able to admit your mess-ups. I fail more than you, but I am not able to admit it. That is what I see as the difference between us."[13] Of course, this enabled Becky to emit a great sigh of relief and gave her a tremendous freedom with her roommate, and with others. When we realize we don't need to put on a show of virtue, we gain the freedom to be ourselves, to be transparent, and this freedom brings great joy.

Jesus continually pointed people to a practice of religion of the heart instead of the externalized rules of the religious leaders of his day.

"Do you not see that whatever goes into a person from outside cannot defile him, since it enters not his heart but his stomach, and is expelled?" (Thus he declared all foods clean.) And he said, "What comes out of a person is what defiles him. For from within, out of the heart of man, come evil thoughts, sexual immorality, theft, murder, adultery, coveting, wickedness, deceit, sensuality, envy, slander, pride, foolishness. All these evil things come from within, and they defile a person." (Mark 7:18–23)

Jesus called his disciples to a sincere expression of faith, which comes from a deep understanding of grace and a heavenly Father who loves us and sees what we do in secret (Matt. 6:4, 18).

No matter how far along we come in our Christian walk, legalism will always be a temptation. It has an attraction. The rules are clear, concrete, unambiguous. If we just had a rule and formula for every situation that might arise in life, it would make things much simpler. But life is not that way. Legalism sucks the joy out of our life. Jesus calls us to live by the Spirit, to understand the spiritual principles, to learn discernment and wisdom that we can apply to whatever circumstances might arise.

The legalistic mindset is portrayed to great effect in the musical *Les Misérables* through the character of Javert, the police inspector who relentlessly pursues Jean Valjean. Valjean spent nineteen years in prison for stealing a loaf of bread but after his release he became a new man, transformed by love and mercy. In the end, after finally catching up with Valjean, Javert cannot bear to live in a world where Valjean is not brought to justice, so he commits suicide by throwing himself into the river Seine.

This might seem like an extreme example, but it is not too far removed from the mindset of the Pharisees who could not rejoice in the blind man's healing because Jesus had healed him on the Sabbath (John 9). The Pharisees were not joyful people, being weighed down by their own rules and self-righteousness.

But we are often tempted to slip back into that "I have to try harder" approach to the Christian life. It calls out to us, luring us back to the yoke of slavery. Don't you sometimes just wish you could stop trying to make yourself look good? I do. It is very tiring.

Tim Keller once commented that his church, Redeemer Presbyterian in Manhattan, on a typical Sunday was made up of one-third seekers, one-third prodigal sons returned home, and one-third elder brothers.[14] Have you ever been in the position of the elder brother, standing on the outside while a party is going on for that wayward brother who has returned home? You are scowling, shouting "unfair!," and are unable to enter into the joy of this happy occasion. I have been there. What a waste. It is no fun.

Eugene Peterson was speaking at an InterVarsity staff conference on the parable of two lost sons (otherwise known as the parable of the prodigal son, Luke 15:11–32). He wanted to make it clear that there are *two* lost sons in this parable. He reflected on the time he was in the hospital for surgery on his leg and got a staph infection, which really set him back and complicated his healing process. He said that just as certain infections, like staph, are usually contracted in the hospital, there are certain sins that are unique to the church. Legalism, or "elder brother-ism," is the infection we are prone to pick up in the church. And we must continually guard against it.

I am very thankful for the grace-centered, gospel-centered preaching in my home church, but I have watched many churches that were once very committed to the gospel of grace lose sight of that foundational truth. They would say they believe we are saved by grace, we are kept by grace, we serve by grace — but in practice they seem to have fallen into a heavy moralism of trying harder. What follows from them is often a judgmental posture on the one hand, or a social gospel mentality on the other that suggests "we can do this," "we can fix this," in response to the deep brokenness in our world, all quite apart from God's power and grace.

There is joy in being a disciple of Jesus, and freedom, and a lightness of spirit. And if we have lost that joy, it must be that somewhere along the way, we got off on a major detour.

Reflection Questions

1. There are many voices in our culture competing for our attention. How might you practice the discipline of listening to the voice of the Good Shepherd (John 10)?

2. We all feel weary at times, tempted to give up the struggle. How are you doing in your fight against sloth (spiritual laziness)? Are there others you know who might need a word of encouragement to stay in the battle (Gal. 6:2, 9)?

3. Anxiety and fear are endemic to our times. Do you find that the tendency to worry often steals your joy? Maybe a daily reading of Matt. 6:25–34 would begin to reshape your worrying habits.

4. Do you find yourself trying to justify yourself, trying to make yourself look good? The temptation of legalistic striving is always lurking in the background of our lives, while God invites us to rest in his gracious love and forgiveness.

8

Joy and Suffering

Perhaps as you've been reading this book about joy, your alarm bells have been going off. "Wait a minute. What about when I am in pain? What about when my mother is dying? What about when my friend has been hospitalized? What about when the whole world is suffering under the COVID-19 pandemic?" I mean, it is fine to write a book about joy when things are just humming along. But what do you say to people who are facing cancer, grieving the loss of a spouse, or saddened by a wayward child?

The crazy thing about it is that I am writing this book about joy as I am presently being treated for bladder cancer, having had four surgeries to remove cancerous growths before finally seeming to bring it under control with treatments. Then recently my wife was diagnosed with breast cancer. And most of this book was written during the COVID lockdowns.

So I am not in a particularly Pollyanna-ish mood as I write these words. My life is not filled with untainted pleasantries, and I am not feeling especially carefree and elated. Nevertheless, I do have an underlying joy at this time in my life, and it is growing. And I do agree that we must seriously address the issue of how we can experience joy in the face of so much suffering in the world and distress in our own lives.

One might think that the most joyful people in the world would be those in the most affluent countries of the West. And that the people who are the most sad and downhearted are from the poorest countries of the "third world." But this is not the case. I have had opportunity to travel to and minister in forty-five countries, and I find the opposite to be true. People in the West are often burdened down, moving at a fast pace, striving for a little bit more and worried about losing what they do have. Whereas some of the most joyful people I have met live in poorer countries. Again and again, I have learned important lessons of faith and joy from brothers and sisters in Africa and Latin America and the former Communist countries of Eastern Europe, even places of severe persecution, social chaos, and deep poverty.

I remember the first time I really read and understood the book of Job. In a strange way I envied Job, because he had lost everything and didn't have to worry about those things being taken away from him; he had nothing more to lose. And he seemed to me to be the freest person I have ever encountered. This is not to minimize his suffering. But the man who has lost everything is a man who no longer fears losing anything. If you compare Job with his speech-giving friends, it is his friends who are the most worried that this same calamity could happen to them. They are desperate to protect their wealth and possessions. They are eager to prove that Job committed some heinous sin. If only they can discover what it was, they will be sure to avoid it. All this is in accordance with their ironclad philosophy of natural retribution, an ancient version of "prosperity theology." But Job was intent on pursuing God. His words keep turning to God in faith and prayer, even in his extreme suffering. In the end, the Almighty honors that faith and reveals himself to Job in a dramatic way. And it is Job who is vindicated and restored by God.

Chapter 8

Joy in the Midst of Suffering

Joy and sorrow are often intertwined. Alexander Schmemann maintains that "the knowledge of the fallen world does not kill joy, which emanates in this world always, constantly, as a bright sorrow."[1] This "bright sorrow," or joyful mourning, for Schmemann and the early church fathers, rightly characterizes the season of Lent, when we experience tears of longing for the glory and peace to come, for the "recovered home" where the Father embraces each of us, his prodigal children, with a boundless depth of forgiving love. In the same way, the sorrow from our sufferings can be mingled with joy because we have a loving heavenly Father who watches over us, cares for us, knows our need, and who is moved by our cries of pain — as he was, for example, when the Israelites called out for deliverance from their bondage in Egypt:

> During those many days the king of Egypt died, and the people of Israel groaned because of their slavery and cried out for help. Their cry for rescue from slavery came up to God. And God heard their groaning, and God remembered his covenant with Abraham, with Isaac, and with Jacob. (Exod. 2:23–24)

God sees our suffering, he hears our groaning, he knows our need, and he responds, not always in immediate deliverance, but in the loving compassion of his presence. He is Immanuel, God with us. The people of Israel certainly may have begun to wonder if God had forgotten them. It had been four hundred years since they left their homeland. And now a pharaoh who "knew not Joseph" had come to power and enslaved them. Their life was burdensome. But God had not forgotten them.

The fact is that when we attempt a careful study of joy in Scripture, we quickly come to realize that suffering and joy appear side by side in the same context, often within the same verse. Generally speaking, in the Old Testament joy comes as a result of being delivered (or with the promise of deliverance) from suffering and hardship.

The psalmist speaks often of how God brings restored joy after suffering:

> Weeping may tarry for the night, but joy comes with the morning. (Ps. 30:6)

> You have turned for me my mourning into dancing; you have loosed my sackcloth and clothed me with gladness. (Ps. 30:11)

Whereas in the New Testament, we find joy in the midst of suffering. Philippians is often called the epistle of joy, and yet Paul was in prison when he wrote it. Marianne Meye Thompson contrasts the "restored joy" in the Old Testament with the "joy notwithstanding" in the New Testament.[2] That is, in the Old Testament, joy is viewed as being restored *after* the time of suffering is over, but in the New Testament, joy is seen to be experienced in the midst of, and in spite of, suffering.

One of the most direct and astonishing statements about joy in suffering comes right at the beginning of James's letter to the scattered Jewish Christians.

> Count it all joy, my brothers, when you meet trials of various kinds, for you know that the testing of your faith produces steadfastness. And let steadfastness have its full effect, that you may be perfect and complete, lacking in nothing. (James 1:2–4)

"Count it all joy"? There was a time when I would have read these words from James and said, "Yeah, right!" And I would have been very dubious about James's grasp of reality. Are we supposed to pretend to be joyful even in the midst of pain and loss? Put on a happy face when my mother is hospitalized, when my best friend is going through a divorce, when fellow believers are martyred for their faith? Does James believe that Christians are immune to hardship?

Clearly, that is not what James has in mind. The believers who would receive his letter were in fact experiencing all manner of persecution, hardship, and loss. They were primarily Jewish Christians who had been scattered abroad due to intense persecution (James 1:1; Acts 8:1–3). Many of them were displaced people, refugees. Some had their property confiscated. Some had been imprisoned. Others were beaten, even martyred. So the "trials" James speaks of are real and intense. Joy is not an escape from suffering. It is not becoming numb to pain. Ann Voskamp writes, "Joy and pain, they are but two arteries of the one heart that pumps through all those that don't numb themselves to real living."[3]

And James is not alone in this teaching about joy in suffering. The great apostles Peter and Paul are of the same persuasion. And Jesus also speaks of joy in persecution. The New Testament is unmistakably clear and consistent about this viewpoint. Consider these bold statements:

But rejoice insofar as you share Christ's sufferings, that you may also rejoice and be glad when his glory is revealed. (1 Pet. 4:13)

Not only that, but we rejoice in our sufferings, knowing that suffering produces endurance, and endurance produces character, and character produces hope, and hope does not put us to shame, because God's love has been poured into our hearts through the Holy Spirit who has been given to us. (Rom. 5:3–5)

"Blessed are those who are persecuted for righteousness' sake, for theirs is the kingdom of heaven.

"Blessed are you when others revile you and persecute you and utter all kinds of evil against you falsely on my account. Rejoice and be glad, for your reward is great in heaven, for so they persecuted the prophets who were before you." (Matt. 5:10–12)

We might be reminded of the incident when Paul and Silas were preaching and healing in the city of Philippi, when a mob turned against them and they were thrown in jail with their feet in stocks (Acts 16:16–24). While in prison, they were praying and singing hymns to God. Such incongruity! There was an earthquake that broke up their chains and the doors flew open, but Paul and Silas remained in their cell. When the jailer saw what happened he cried out, "What must I do to be saved?" They replied, "Believe on the Lord Jesus Christ and you shall be saved, you and your household." The jailer and his household believed and were baptized, and they rejoiced greatly (Acts 16:34).

What are we to make of all these passages?

First of all, the Bible is very realistic and honest about pain and suffering. The Christian faith is not one that suggests that pain is an illusion, a figment of your imagination. It does not downplay the significance of pain and loss. It looks suffering squarely in the face and still can rejoice. Pain is real, trouble will come, suffering is inevitable, but *misery is a choice.*

Tim Keller, in his book on suffering, doesn't pull any punches about the reality and inevitability of suffering:

Suffering is everywhere, unavoidable, and its scope often overwhelms. . . . Death is irreducibly unpredictable and unavoidable. . . . The loss of loved ones, debilitating and fatal illnesses, personal betrayals, financial reversals, and moral failures — all of these will eventually come upon you if you live out a normal life span. No one is immune. . . . Human life is fatally fragile and subject to forces beyond our power to manage. Life is tragic.[4]

It is one of the unique tenets of Christian teaching that evil and suffering are real and pervasive in our world. This recognition of evil was the main reason psychiatrist Scott Peck was initially drawn to the Christian faith, after twenty years in Zen Buddhism.[5] This world is dark and broken and hurting. And this is not the way it is supposed to be. So these New Testament claims that we can know joy in the midst of suffering are not just a case of bad psychology stemming from a denial of the reality of suffering. The Old Testament also takes an honest and realistic view of suffering. The stories are fully human in their depiction of pain and sorrow and loss. Close to 60 percent of the Psalms have elements of very honest lament. But they almost always conclude with praise and rejoicing and thanksgiving.

An Alternative Interpretation of Suffering

One key to understanding this seeming contradiction is in that word "count" it or "consider" it to be joy (James 1:2).[6] Paul "considers" all his Jewish pedigree and status to be rubbish in comparison with the surpassing worth of knowing Christ Jesus (Phil. 3:7–11). Similarly, Peter views the delay of the Lord's return as God's patience, not desiring that any should perish (1 Pet. 3:9). It puts a whole different light on the same set of facts. Jesus did not "consider" equality with God something to be grasped but emptied himself (Phil. 2:6). The same idea is sometimes expressed, without the use of the word "consider." A woman in labor looks back on the pains of childbirth differently "because of her joy that a child is born into the world" (John 16:21 NIV). And Jesus "for the joy that was set before him endured the cross, despising the shame, and is seated at the right hand of the throne of God" (Heb. 12:2). He certainly experienced the pain of the cross, but he offered himself gladly because of the tremendous redemptive outcome — our salvation.

As long as we are consumed with our affliction, unable to see any purpose or meaning in our suffering and unwilling to consider God's presence and his perspective on our loss, we will miss out on the value that suffering can bring to our lives.

For Christians, there is a spiritual reality that influences the way we view our experience of pain and suffering. It is clear that there are differing ways of interpreting the same set of facts or circumstances. So, what is this different perspective, this alternative viewpoint that can allow us to "rejoice in our sufferings"? There is certainly a joy that comes when we experience relief or healing from our afflictions. But the joy that can be ours in the crucible of suffering comes from an understanding that these trials do not signal the absence of God, but rather a wonderful awareness of his presence and comfort, and a confidence that he can use the trials for our good.

When we are suffering and, like Job, we cry out, "Why?," we don't really want some philosophical explanation, some rational understanding. What Job needed, and what we need, is to know God's presence, to know that he cares, that he has not abandoned us. The Almighty finally speaks to Job in the thunderstorm. And Job is strangely at peace: "I had heard of you by the hearing of the ear, but now my eye sees you" (Job 42:5). We have this same assurance because our God cared so much that he entered our world, took on our flesh, experienced our suffering, and died our death (Phil. 2:5-11).

What I hope is clear by now is that I am not suggesting any denial or pretending about our circumstances. When James says, "Count it all joy," he is not suggesting that his fellow believers pretend that the pain is not real, or that they should deny the reality of their present circumstances. Rather, he is appealing to them to take a different view of this real suffering — not simply an eternal viewpoint (though that is part of it) but a divine understanding. What is

God doing in this? How is God present in this? What possible meaning or purpose could this have? How could this adversity be used to transform my character? How might God help me to respond to this suffering in a healthy, honest, and redemptive manner?

So, on a practical level, how can we still have joy in the midst of suffering? First, let's learn from one person's story.

The Joni Eareckson Tada Story

If you want to gain understanding about suffering, don't consult the armchair philosophers; don't listen to those who are just angry about all the people who are suffering in the world. Listen to those who have actually suffered, and suffered greatly, but are still living a life of faith and patient obedience. I was at first inclined to reference a different story, because everyone seems to cite Joni Eareckson Tada. But as I reread her story, I was won over, not just because it is such a dramatic story, but because her understanding coming out of her suffering is so profound.

Many of us know her story. Joni was injured in a diving accident in 1967 at age seventeen, when she misjudged the depth of the water in the Chesapeake Bay. It fractured her spine, broke her neck, and left her paralyzed from the neck down. Joni loved life, loved to swim, and wholeheartedly pursued other sports, following her father's example (an Olympic-level wrestler). Suddenly her whole life was turned upside down; she was a quadriplegic. She went through two years of rehab, with deep anger, confusion, depression, and doubt about God. She felt that her life was over. She begged her friends to help her commit suicide, since she was unable to do it herself. Many well-meaning friends offered her pious clichés and naive comments that just seemed to trivialize her plight and increased her suffering.

Joni had a vague idea that there may be some answers in the Bible, but she needed someone who could help her find them. She finally asked a friend, a young man named Steve, if he could tell her why this had happened to her. If God is all-powerful and all-loving, why has this happened? Steve was understandably daunted by this request. It is a question that has puzzled many learned theologians. But Steve just pointed her to Jesus's example, especially his suffering and death for us. God took what the rulers of this world meant for evil and made it into a miracle that brought an incredible amount of good, our salvation. The world's worst murder became the world's only salvation. And that is what God does. Yes, God is in control. Wisely, Steve just left it there and allowed time for it to sink in — that perhaps God could do something miraculous in Joni's life through this terrible suffering.

There are two perspectives on what happened to Joni Eareckson Tada, and both are true. On the one hand, it was a reckless, tragic accident — a careless dive into shallow water — that left her paralyzed. All her hopes and dreams in life were dashed, her family was shattered, and at least it appeared that her faith was destroyed. For many, that is the only perspective. On the other hand, in Joni's words,

> God's plan in the accident in which I became paralyzed, His purpose was to turn a head strong stubborn rebellious kid into a young woman who would reflect something of patience, something of endurance, something of longsuffering, who would get her life values turned from wrong side down to right side up and would have a buoyant and lively optimistic hope of heavenly glories above.[7]

While there is not inherent goodness in a crippling diving accident, or disease, or deformity, God can and does bring about great good out of the ashes of such tragic loss.

The rest is history. Joni became a lifelong devoted follower of Jesus Christ. She went on to write over forty books, recorded several music albums, became an artist (with a paintbrush in her mouth), starred in an autobiographical movie, and has become a leading advocate for people with disabilities. In 1979 she established her ministry, Joni and Friends, lecturing around the world at retreats and conferences.

Finding Joy in Suffering?

Now let's draw on some principles from Joni Eareckson Tada's story and bring it together with the Bible's teaching on suffering.

1. God's promise is to be with us in our suffering and loss.

God has not promised to shield us from pain and suffering and even death. But he does promise to be with us in every time of temptation and in every need. Jesus comes to our side as one who has also suffered much, even to death, and who can sympathize with our weakness and sorrow. He shared in our flesh and blood, he laid aside his immunity to sickness, sorrow, grief, humiliation, and death itself (Phil. 2:6–8). He is our great high priest. He will not abandon us in our time of need, even though we may feel that he has. Jesus walked this way before us and is able to understand our pain. And his presence brings us joy.

> Since then we have a great high priest who has passed through the heavens, Jesus, the Son of God, let us hold fast our confession. For we do not have a high priest who is unable to sympathize with our weaknesses, but one who in every respect has been tempted as we are, yet without sin. Let us then with confidence draw near to the throne of grace, that we may receive mercy and find grace to help in time of need. (Heb. 4:14–16)

Since therefore the children share in flesh and blood, he himself likewise partook of the same things. . . . For because he himself has suffered when tempted, he is able to help those who are being tempted. (Heb. 2:14, 18)

In Joni Eareckson Tada's words, "God has not healed me, but he holds me." In her hospital room, after her accident, she says this:

I pictured Jesus. I didn't see Him and there were no visions, but I imagined Him coming to visit me. It was dark and He tiptoed past my sleeping roommates, and I sensed Him lowering the guardrail of my hospital bed and sitting on the edge of my mattress, and with one hand leaning over to brush back my hair, and with the other hand showing me His nail print in His palm, looking at me and saying, "Joni, if I loved you enough to die for you, then don't you think I can be trusted — even with this?"[8]

2. *In all these things, God is still working for our good.*

Romans 8:28 is often quoted, and often seems hollow and empty, during times of deep suffering: "And we know that for those who love God all things work together for good, for those who are called according to his purpose." Can my cancer be good? Can my child's death be good? No, these things are an evil and a blight on God's good creation. But even in these distortions of God's good design for his world, he is working all things for good.

We rarely can see at the time of our pain how in the world this can become something good. And we may not see it in our lifetime. How could Joni's terrible injury be used to work something good? Once again, her words:

You know, God is an expert at exchanging the meaning of awful things and giving those awful things new fresh meaning — hopeful meaning. I mean, look at what He did at the cross. I mean right there, a symbol of torture, of murder, of carnage and grief, of unthinkable suffering and hardship. God exchanged the meaning of the cross to something that is now hopeful, and victorious, and joyful, and full of meaning.

And I look at my wheelchair the same way. Just like God turned water into wine, He turned this wheelchair into a classroom, as it were. He exchanged the meaning for it. Because if you look at a wheelchair, most people think you're confined, you are imprisoned. But hey, with Jesus, this is the prison that has set me free, and I'm not confined to a wheelchair. Oh sure, I might be a wheelchair user, but my wheelchair is this classroom which God has instructed me on how to trust Him in the hard places.[9]

We look at Joni in her wheelchair and see confinement, limitation, but she has come to see her wheelchair as a "classroom" where God has taught her, and so many others, the most important lessons about life. Her wheelchair has become her salvation and has set her free. You can scoff at this story and her interpretation and call it naive. But she has been living this reality now for fifty years. She is a joyful person. She has lived a much fuller life than she could have imagined before her accident. Her earlier hopes and dreams pale in comparison to the life God has given her.

3. *God uses suffering to reshape our character, our values, and our priorities.*

Paul rejoices in sufferings because they are able to produce perseverance, character, and hope (Rom. 5:3–5). Once again, we may not see it at the time. But often, as we look back, we can see how this suffering has shaped our character in ways that would not have been otherwise possible. It purifies our thoughts, and it reminds us what is important in life. It is, as C. S. Lewis suggests, God's megaphone. "God whispers to us in our pleasures, speaks in our conscience, but shouts in our pain: it is His megaphone to rouse a deaf world."[10]

Once again, let's let Joni be our wise teacher:

> God used this injury to develop in me patience and endurance and tolerance and self-control and steadfastness and sensitivity and love and joy. There was a time when I used to think that man's chief end for happiness was to have a date on Friday night and to be a slim trim 135 lbs, a size 12 dress, a college degree, a nice little home in suburbia with a white picket fence with Ethan Allen furniture, and 2.5 children. That's what I used to think was important in life. After my accident, those life values got turned around and I began to see that what really mattered in life were friendships. What really mattered in life was love, warm and deep and real and personal, between a husband and a wife, or a sister, or a brother, or an aunt, or a niece, or a nephew, or a neighbor, or a nurse, or an attendant. I began to see that it was people who counted. And smiles and tears and embraces, these things began to count so much in my life.[11]

There are no meaningless events, no chance accidents that come into our life. Life is not just one big ridiculous absurdity. This world has meaning because God is sovereign, and he is guiding its future.

One of the most grievous consequences of our secular society, which moves God to the margins, if not totally out of the picture, is that there is no meaning for evil, pain, and suffering. As Tim Keller points out, every culture has an obligation to its citizens to offer some explanation to the biggest questions and problems of life. If it does not, it is, and should be, eventually disqualified.[12] Our secular Western society has perhaps the weakest response to suffering of any culture in history. For the average person in the West, suffering is little more than a rude interruption to our lives and plans. The medical community is responsible to fix it and make it go away. This is not an honest response. It doesn't correspond to our reality. And it does not offer hope and joy in the midst of suffering; you must only grit your teeth and bear it.

4. *Trials refine and purify our faith.*

Every hardship and adversity that comes our way also acts as a trial, a test of our faith. A colleague recently told of how his team of InterVarsity staff had spent several hours together studying 1 Peter. He wrote, "As we studied 1 Peter together, we discerned that Christian resilience is the ability to receive adversity as a force to refine our faith."

> In this you rejoice, though now for a little while, if necessary, you have been grieved by various trials, so that the tested genuineness of your faith — more precious than gold that perishes though it is tested by fire — may be found to result in praise and glory and honor at the revelation of Jesus Christ. (1 Pet. 1:6–7)

The prophet Malachi also spoke of this cleansing and refining work of God:

> But who can endure the day of his coming, and who can stand when he appears? For he is like a refiner's fire and like fullers' soap. He will sit as a refiner and purifier of silver, and he will pu-

rify the sons of Levi and refine them like gold and silver, and they will bring offerings in righteousness to the LORD. (Mal. 3:2–3)

I have often asked God that in whatever trials he allows into my life, he would also give me the grace to remain faithful. Viewing our adversity in this way can add joy to our lives, even in the midst of suffering.

The hymn writer captures this truth in "How Firm a Foundation":

> When through fiery trials thy pathway shall lie,
> my grace, all-sufficient, shall be thy supply.
> The flame shall not hurt thee; I only design
> thy dross to consume, and thy gold to refine.

But there is no point trying to imagine how we would respond if some calamity does happen to us. It hasn't happened yet, and God has not given us the grace we will need for that moment yet. An old preacher was asked if he had the grace to withstand a great loss like the death of a child. His wise response was "No, I don't have enough grace to withstand that trial, because it hasn't happened yet, and God has not yet given me the grace for that trial. When and if it does come upon me, then his grace will be sufficient."

5. *Our earthly life is brief compared to eternity.*

> So, we do not lose heart. Though our outer self is wasting away, our inner self is being renewed day by day. For this light momentary affliction is preparing for us an eternal weight of glory beyond all comparison, as we look not to the things that are

seen but to the things that are unseen. For the things that are
seen are transient, but the things that are unseen are eternal.
(2 Cor. 4:16–18)

For I consider that the sufferings of this present time are not
worth comparing with the glory that is to be revealed to us.
(Rom. 8:18)

When I was twenty-five years old, I was certainly not thinking
about the brevity of life. Now that I am in my senior years, my
mortality is much more real, and life seems much more fragile and
brief. And the hope of glory is ever nearer. Have you noticed when
talking with dear saints who are nearing the end of their earthly
journey, that their interest in the affairs of this world is fading, and
their thoughts are much more occupied with the next chapter of
their life – glory?

In the Corinthians passage above, Paul draws out two contrasts
between life on earth and life in heaven. First, the length of time.
What is seventy or eighty years compared to eternity? Second, the
quality of life. Our earthly afflictions (and Paul had many) cannot
be compared with the "eternal weight of glory." If you put them on
a scale – this earthly life and eternal glory – then clearly eternal
glory far outweighs this life. This is not, however, to trivialize the
suffering (see 2 Cor. 4:8–12).

C. S. Lewis delivered an entire sermon on the phrase "the
weight of glory" right in the middle of World War II, in 1941.[13] The
prospect of actually sharing in God's eternal glory is so far beyond
our comprehension that it feels like a heavy weight.

To please God . . . to be a real ingredient in the divine happiness
. . . to be loved by God, not merely pitied, but delighted in as an

artist delights in his work or a father in a son — it seems impossible, a weight or burden of glory which our thoughts can hardly sustain. But so it is. . . . For glory means good report with God, acceptance by God, response, acknowledgement, and welcome into the heart of things. The door on which we have been knocking all our lives will open to us.[14]

Once again, here is a word from Joni:

I just don't want to give the gospel; I want to embody the gospel. I want to become the gospel to people like that who are despairing of their suffering and their affliction. I want to let them know there is hope. That hope really can be found in Jesus Christ, and that hope can take any assault from the enemy, every disappointment, every discouragement. I want to tell people that when every darkness and desolation occurs, to embrace it with both hands as a blessed opportunity to die to yourself and live more fully to Jesus Christ.[15]

Alternatives to a Joyful Response

There are other ways to respond to suffering that are less noble and redemptive, and far too many people choose these destructive responses.

Bitterness and resentment can swallow people up in the face of extreme suffering and loss. When I was a young pastor in a small town, I was asked to call on Mr. White, who had lost his sixteen-year-old son in a car accident several years ago. He was bitter and refused to have anything to do with church. He rarely even left the house. I visited him. He hardly looked at me but said, "Reverend, I don't want any part of a God who would let this happen to my son." I tried to talk with him, to tell him that God had also lost his son, that God grieves with him over his loss, and that his son is in the arms of Jesus. But he would have none of it. His heart was closed. And he ultimately died a very bitter old man.

A few years later, my longtime friend Bill also lost his sixteen-year-old son in a car accident. God's grace enveloped Bill immediately. He was thanking and comforting the young nurse who had to share this news with him over the phone, and he was comforting the rest of us at the memorial service. Sure, he was grieving, and he shared many touching stories about his son whom he would sorely miss. As time went on, Bill had a ministry to many people who had lost a child. When he heard of someone in the community who had suffered this particular loss, he would often call them on the phone and share his story and offer to pray with them.

What a difference between these two men. One who refused to allow God's healing grace into his life. The other who began to experience God's healing very soon and continued on that path. One who preferred to nurse his grudge against God and hold on to resentment. The other who opened his arms to God and turned this loss into an opportunity to minister to others. One who had lost his faith. The other whose faith was tested and purified like gold and grew in stature, to the extent that this friend is one of the heroes of faith in the cloud of witnesses in Hebrews 11.

Others respond to loss by lapsing into denial, which is really detrimental to our mental health — to respond with "This can't be happening to me" or, even worse, "This didn't happen to me." My family and I ministered in the West African country of Liberia for a summer. As a result of this experience, we formed a close friendship with a Liberian family, the Wesleys, who were involved in leading a student ministry in that country. Soon after our visit, Liberia fell into a civil war led by the infamous Charles Taylor. We were able to help this family receive asylum in the US, and they lived with us for a while. They shared that so many people lost everything in the war — their homes, their livelihood, family members. Some accepted this loss with strong faith in God. Others could not accept it, could not believe it, and our friends told us that many of those others lost their sanity in the process of this denial.

More often, people just lapse into a sort of passive resignation, and gradually move on with their lives. What a lot of wasted suffering that could have been so profitable in building our character, purifying and deepening our faith, waking us up to what is truly important in life, and catalyzing our ministry to others. People like my friend Bill and Joni Eareckson Tada have shown us a better way.

God has something far better for us. He is preparing us for an eternity when we will finally enter his land, where there is no more crying or dying or sighing, a land of love and light and life as it should be, because we are destined for joy.

Reflection Questions

1. Christians are not immune to hardship. Is this a time of intense suffering in your life? Is it really possible to have joy, even in the midst of suffering (James 1:2–4)?

2. What is your first response when hard things come into your life? Does it take you by surprise? We may be tempted to deny it or reject it. Scripture is clear that we live in a broken world. Pain and suffering are real and inevitable. Can you rest in God's promise to be with us in our time of need (Heb. 4:14–16)?

3. Could you begin to reinterpret these difficult circumstances (count it, consider it differently)? Could you view them as times of testing, opportunities for growth and maturity?

4. How has God used suffering to reshape your character and values? Can you trust him to use present hardship to refine and purify you?

5. What are some lessons you can learn from the Joni Eareckson Tada story?

9

Joy in Service

What is a wasted life? What is the good life? What makes life worth living? There are countless self-help books, articles, and podcasts on how not to waste your life. "Ten signs you are wasting your life." "Quit doing these six things today." "Eight things successful people don't do." "You may be wasting your life with the wrong marriage partner." "You may be wasting your life in the wrong job."

What seems clear in the popular notion is that the self-fulfilled, self-actualized life is the best life. It is doing what you want to do in life and doing it your own way. We are led to believe that if you can come to the end of your life and say, as in the Frank Sinatra song, "I did it my way," then you will not have wasted your life. This is the model of a successful life promoted in much of our culture.

In 1885 six of the brightest Cambridge University graduates, and one from the Royal Military Academy, decided to give up the promise of prestigious careers and become missionaries to China. They are still known as the Cambridge Seven. It was during the height of the prosperous reign of Queen Victoria, and not many university students were interested in missions. The English church had become largely lethargic. Hudson Taylor's mission to the interior of

China was still not well known. Ministering to the poor in China's rural districts, where disease was common and the people were unlearned, was not considered a glamorous calling. And yet this was the vocation that these young men believed God was calling them to. Many of them did contract disease, and some died in China. Many of their friends and families back in England thought they were wasting their lives, throwing away good careers as surgeons, attorneys, and businessmen to serve in some obscure village in China.

Perhaps the best-known of these Cambridge Seven was Charles T. Studd. Charles loved the game of cricket and was becoming one of the best cricketers in England. He was captain of the Eton cricket team, then captain of the Cambridge cricket team. By then, he had become famous as one of the greatest cricket players in the country, and he was the sports idol of schoolboys. But his heart had turned cold toward Jesus. It was when his younger brother, George, lay dying that Charles was shaken and began to ask himself, "Now what is all the popularity of the world to George? What is all the fame and flattering? What is it worth to possess the riches of the world, when a man comes to face Eternity?" He went to hear Dwight L. Moody preach at one of his London evangelistic missions and gave his life to Christ. "There the Lord met me again and restored to me the joy of His salvation. Still further, and what was better than all, He set me to work for Him."[1]

Giving Yourself Away?

Remember the words of the Lord Jesus, how he himself said, "It is more blessed to give than to receive." (Acts 20:35)

The apostle Paul quoted these words of Jesus (not found in the Gospel accounts) to the Ephesian elders just before his departure to Rome. They were indeed important words to remember.

I have already noted that the word "blessed" is closely associated with joy. So we could also say it is more *joyful* to give than to receive. In saying this, Jesus was calling his followers out of a life of self-serving and self-gratification. There is no joy to be found there, only short-lived pleasures. We are called to sacrificial giving of ourselves to others. This is, ironically, the real path of joy.

David Brooks states it this way:

> Joy is found on the far side of sacrificial service. It is found in giving yourself away. When you see that, you realize that joy is not just a feeling, it is a moral outlook. It is a permanent state of thanksgiving and friendship, communion and solidarity.[2]

This may all be counterintuitive to us. Our culture surely seems to suggest that happiness is to be found in piling up our possessions, then trading them in for better ones. It is to be found in chasing after the most exciting experiences money can buy. In the end, the one with the most toys wins. Wins what?

Harvey Cox from Harvard once said, in contrasting the gluttony of food with the gluttony of experiences, that at least the gluttony of food has limits, in that our physical hunger can be satiated.[3] We can only eat so much food before we become sick. But the gluttony of experiences has no end or boundaries; this hunger is insatiable. There is always another exciting experience out there that we simply must take hold of or we will feel somehow cheated and diminished. Cox reminds us that Saint John of the Cross warned against the covetousness of the soul and preached that it could be even *more* dangerous than the body's voraciousness.[4] This is all reminiscent of Jesus's saying "For what will it profit a man if he gains the whole world and forfeits his soul? Or what shall a man give in return for his soul?" (Matt. 16:26). Many people believe that joy is to be found in a family trip to Disney World, or to some exotic island. But these experiences are short-lived and usually don't measure up to our expectations, perhaps because we are expecting too much from them. Others hope that being married and having children, living in the proverbial house with a white picket fence will bring them supreme happiness. But even marriage and family, which are good gifts from God, become idolatry when we try to make them our ultimate end in life. It will disappoint us. We will hold onto it too tightly and strangle the life out of it.

But there is real joy in giving ourselves away. Real joy comes in using our God-given abilities and energies in serving others. We find our greatest joy by joining with a community of like-minded people to do something beautiful for God, by caring for his creation and his people, especially the poor.

Something Beautiful for God

Malcolm Muggeridge, the quintessential skeptic and BBC foreign correspondent, went to visit Mother Teresa in Calcutta for an interview in 1967. He was so impressed by her ministry that he returned with a BBC film crew to do a full documentary. Muggeridge eventually converted to Christianity, and later joined the Roman Catholic Church, largely because of the influence of Mother Teresa.

Muggeridge details his encounter with Mother Teresa in his book *Something Beautiful for God*,[5] where he describes her as a "light which could never be extinguished." He was continually astonished by the Missionaries of Charity, the order of sisters Mother Teresa founded, and by the Home for the Dying they had set up. One surprising discovery was that the halls "rang with laughter" as the sisters ministered to the severely injured, the sick, and the dying people they had picked up from the streets of Calcutta. Muggeridge says, "It is not the bare house in a dark slum that is conjured up in my mind, but a light shining and a joy abounding."[6] He quotes Mother Teresa: "We give it and we do it to God, to Christ, and that's why we try to do it as beautifully as possible."[7] Mother Teresa lived her life following the two greatest commandments: to love God and to love our neighbors. Muggeridge left this place happy. And he soon entered the most joyful time of his life with his new-found faith in Christ, described in *Jesus Rediscovered*.[8]

Mother Teresa, in spite of her growing popularity, especially after the BBC documentary, retained her joyful humility, still cleaning the toilets in the Home for the Dying until she was too sick to do so. I was ministering with students in the 1990s in what is now called North Macedonia (former Yugoslavia), Mother Teresa's home country. In its capital city of Skopje, I came across a small plaque on the pavement near a busy street, stating that "Mother Teresa of Calcutta was born here." No great monument, just a small reminder of her humble beginnings. She was not celebrated by the Macedonians because she was part of the country's Albanian minority, a perceived threat. And she was not celebrated by her fellow Albanians because they are predominantly Muslim, and she of course was Catholic.

My family and I were living in Oxford in 1997 when Princess Diana was killed in that terrible car crash. It was the day of the funeral. All the shops were closed for the day. Everyone seemed to be in a state of grief and shock. I picked up a local newspaper, with photos of Diana covering the front page. Then I noticed a small paragraph at the bottom, very inconspicuous, that read, "Mother Teresa died today." And I thought, "How appropriate that this great lady, this faithful, lifelong servant of Christ, should die with such little recognition, overshadowed by the funeral of a princess. This is how she would have wanted it."

The joyful life is one in which we give ourselves away. In the call to discipleship, Jesus made the paradoxical statement "For whoever would save his life will lose it, but whoever loses his life for my sake will find it" (Matt. 16:25). It is so true. When we try to hang on to our life, to protect our time, to shield our privacy, to pursue our self-centered ambitions, we miss out on real life and we lose our joy. When we offer our life for the sake of Christ and for the "least of these," we find great joy and fulfillment. Rather than being afraid that we will be used up, rather than being stingy with our time and attention, we are set free to give of ourselves for others. There is certainly a need for boundaries; we cannot simply drive ourselves to exhaustion and neglect our health. But boundaries can quickly become walls of self-protectiveness, and this is not the way to joy. Jesus is our example in giving himself away to the sick and needy. Yes, he took time to find a quiet place for rest and prayer. But he worked tirelessly, entering into people's lives, mingling with their pain and their joys.

A Generous Spirit

The life of generosity is a joyful life. We don't find joy from a self-protective, hoarding, zero-sum, scarcity attitude toward life. We find it in the magnanimous outlook that we see in the life of Abraham, for example. In Genesis 13, he and his nephew Lot come to the Negev, and their flocks and herds had grown to the extent that it was causing friction between their herders. Abraham's generous solution is to give Lot his first choice of which land to possess.

> "Let there be no strife between you and me, and between your herdsmen and my herdsmen, for we are kinsmen. Is not the whole land before you? Separate yourself from me. If you take the left hand, then I will go to the right, or if you take the right hand, then I will go to the left." (Gen. 13:8–9)

The young Lot chooses the fertile, well-watered land along the Jordan River valley. This turns out to be a disaster for Lot, because it leads him to the wicked city of Sodom. Yet, when Lot and his family find themselves taken captive after a lost battle between the kings of Sodom and Gomorrah against five other kings, it is Abraham who comes with a small army to rescue Lot (Gen. 14). Then again, when the Lord's judgment comes against the evil cities of Sodom and Gomorrah to destroy them, Abraham is magnanimous in interceding with the Lord for Lot and his family, and they are rescued out of the burning city (Gen. 18–19).

We see this principle in action in the New Testament also when the Macedonian believers give joyfully and generously of their own resources, without any thought to themselves.

> For in a severe test of affliction, their abundance of joy and their extreme poverty have overflowed in a wealth of generosity on their part. For they gave according to their means, as I can testify, and beyond their means, of their own accord, begging us earnestly for the favor of taking part in the relief of the saints. (2 Cor. 8:2–4)

Serving Together

This is not an individualistic, lone-wolf call to service. From the very beginning, Jesus called a group of disciples to serve together with him as a team. He sent them out on missions into towns and villages, doing the same kind of ministry he had demonstrated. This was not going to be one-man show. Of course, in Jesus's redemptive work on the cross, he alone could accomplish this. But as for ministry, that was always carried out in community. There was a band of disciples, men and women whose lives had been changed, who traveled with him everywhere he went. From the start he was building his "little flock," he was forming a new community, he was establishing his church — a people of God who would be the beginning of a new kind of kingdom of sacrificial love and joyful service (Luke 12:32). When the seventy-two disciples returned from their mission in the villages, Jesus "rejoiced in the Holy Spirit and said, 'I thank you, Father, Lord of heaven and earth, that you have hidden these things from the wise and understanding and revealed them to little children; yes, Father, for such was your gracious will'" (Luke 10:21).

Paul rejoices continually for those who shared with him in the partnership in the gospel. It is no wonder that his letter to the church at Philippi is called the epistle of joy. Even when Paul was in prison, he was aware of this church's concern for him and their support of him. He was not alone in this mission. This was a team effort.

> What then? Only that in every way, whether in pretense or in truth, Christ is proclaimed, and in that I rejoice. Yes, and I will rejoice, for I know that through your prayers and the help of the Spirit of Jesus Christ this will turn out for my deliverance. (Phil. 1:18–19)

> I rejoiced in the Lord greatly that now at length you have revived your concern for me. You were indeed concerned for me, but you had no opportunity. (Phil. 4:10)

There is joy in serving Jesus, and freedom (John 8:36). As I've said earlier, if life has become a burdensome grind of mere existence, a dull and joyless drudgery, we must begin to ask ourselves some searching questions. Is it still Jesus I am following and serving? Have I taken on burdens that God never intended for me to bear? Have I taken my eyes off the Lord and now find myself drowning, as Peter did? Have I assumed a "messiah complex," setting myself up as the be-all and end-all of a human project? Where is it that I got off the path of joyful service? How did I lose that lightness in my spirit? How can I regain the joy?

Gospel-Centered Service

1. The Joy of Not Playing God

We can regain joy and freedom in our service when we recognize some foundational truths. One essential to remember is that God is God and we are not. When Chevy Chase used to give the "news" on *Saturday Night Live*, he would begin with "Hello, I am Chevy Chase . . . and you're not." Sometimes I think God needs to say to us, "Hello, I am God, and you're not." Thankfully, we serve a great and powerful God who delights to work through the prayers and loving care of his people. We need not, and must not, take all the burdens of the world on our shoulders. It may be a great boost to our ego to think we can be the savior for hurting people, but it is deadly and futile. Our greatest strength, ironically, is an awareness of our dependence on God and others.

A colleague and friend once shared an experience from his own life that illustrates this well. He was serving InterVarsity in a leadership role in New England. One evening he was at home with his family, and he and his wife were having a hard conversation about his schedule. She was in tears, and they were working on it. Just then the doorbell rang. He answered, and it was a student leader from the InterVarsity fellowship in another city. She was in tears. She had traveled a long way to talk with him about a problem. He stood in the doorway. He was facing the student who was in tears. He turned around and saw his wife, also in tears. In that moment, he made a crucial decision. He said to the student, "I am sorry, I cannot talk with you tonight." He gave her the information of a local student leader who could give her a place to stay, and he offered to see her the next day. She was somewhat surprised, but she left. He turned around and continued the conversation with his wife. You can imagine how affirming that decision was for his wife, and they quickly worked through their conflict about his schedule. The next day, when he spoke to the student leader, she was in a much more buoyant mood and said to him, "Thank you for not talking with me last night. What I really needed was to talk to God about my problem. I did that and found resolution and peace." It was a lesson he never forgot.

In Mark 4, we have a great example of a community of friends working together. Jesus is preaching and healing at his home in Capernaum, with large crowds surrounding the house such that no one else could enter. Suddenly the crowd is startled to see a group of friends lowering a paralyzed man on his bed, through the roof, into the room where Jesus is teaching. It must have been a comical scene. But it says, "When Jesus saw *their* faith, he said to the paralytic, 'Son, your sins are forgiven'" (Mark 4:5, emphasis mine). Later Jesus tells him to get up and walk. What is striking is how dependent this man was upon his friends, who loved him enough to attempt such a daring deed, and also how this man acted on their belief that Jesus could heal him. The man was also completely dependent on Jesus — first, to know forgiveness of his sins, and second, to receive physical healing.

2. *The Deeper Magic*

Another foundational truth of joyful service is that the gospel is our message and our ministry; the gospel is powerful, and the gospel is good news (Rom. 1:16; 1 Cor. 1:17–19). It is not our clever arguments or our strategic thinking or our ability to influence people. The gospel may seem to be folly to the world, but it is the wisdom of God. It is wiser than the wise. To borrow Lewis's phrase from the Narnia tales, it represents a "deeper magic." It has the power to change lives, to bring about true redemption. We are called not only to meet people in their pain but also to offer supernatural deliverance. There is so much crying need in the world, that without God's intervention, our task would indeed be hopeless. We are called not simply to help people cope with their pain and suffering but to help them flourish. Our ministry is therefore a joyful one, not a drudgery. We expect miracles, we ask God for miracles. When I consider the miracle God has accomplished in my own life in graciously calling me out, in transforming me, in healing me, and the work he is still doing in me, it gives me hope that he is also at work in the lives of others.

Mary Clark Moschella, professor of pastoral care and counseling at Yale Divinity School, points out that with few exceptions, joy has tended to be a neglected area of interest in the caregiving professions, which includes counselors, social workers, pastors, and psychologists. Pastoral counseling, for example, is often viewed as the practice of dealing with human suffering, taking a problem-centered approach. As a result, the focus tends to be on coping and surviving, not on flourishing or helping people move toward joy. But as we have seen, suffering and joy are not opposites, but often close companions. Tears of sorrow are often mingled with tears of joy. Moschella says "we have attended more to the agony than ecstasy" when caring for people in need, and she calls for a new methodology of "making room for joy."[9] The predominant negative approach tends to undervalue what it means to be fully human. It also underestimates the power of God to intervene in our caregiving and to achieve a much greater end than we, with our limited viewpoint, might expect. Joy is in fact linked to pointing people to God's goodness and mercy, and to reminding people of God's promises and intentions for us. This can be a life-giving ministry if we are willing to communicate the gospel to people at their point of need.

3. Nobody Is a Nobody

Another essential truth is that every person is made in the image and likeness of God, regardless of race, color, ethnicity, age, gender, stature, appearance, ability or disability, or economic standing (Gen. 1:27–28). Nobody is a nobody. Every person has dignity and value before God. Every person is a somebody. We are called to serve as God's representatives, and the consistent biblical teaching is that God "shows no partiality" and therefore we must show no partiality, no favoritism, no discrimination (Acts 10:34; Rom. 2:11; Eph. 6:9; 1 Tim. 5:21; James 2:1).

Richard John Neuhaus stated it so eloquently:

> We contend, and we contend relentlessly, for the dignity of the human person, of every human person created in the image and likeness of God, . . . every human person, no matter how weak or how strong, no matter how young or how old, no matter how productive or how burdensome, no matter how welcome or how inconvenient.[10]

It was an emotional moment at the 2020 Emmy Awards ceremony when Demi Lovato, who had been off the stage for two years and who had suffered a drug overdose and been hospitalized, now returned to the stage to sing her newly released song "Anyone." With tears streaming down her face, and having to restart the song, struggling to keep her composure, she sang about how she poured out her heart through music, to shooting stars, and into alcohol, but no one seemed to hear her. "Anyone, please send me anyone / Lord, is there anyone? / I need someone." Lovato apparently wrote this song just before the overdose that almost finished her. How many other cries for help must there be that never make their way into a song? How many others feel that nobody is listening? How many are crying out, "Lord, is there anyone? Is there someone who will listen, someone who will care?"

Someone who does care is medical doctor Paul Farmer (1959–2022), who spent a lifetime serving the poor in Haiti. In *Mountains Beyond Mountains*, Tracy Kidder tells Farmer's story, lifting him up as an example of someone who serves with joy.[11] In Haiti Farmer founded Partners in Health, a ministry now operating in several countries around the world, treating HIV/AIDS and other diseases. He worked tirelessly to help prevent what he called "stupid deaths" that could be easily prevented by appropriate health care. Mary Clark Moschella believes the secret to the joy and gratitude evident in Farmer's life and work, even in the face of immense suffering, was his notion of the good — he did not believe the good is a scarce commodity.[12]

4. Whistle While You Work?

God's good creation gift of work is a mixed bag today. Let's face it: we humans have a love-hate relationship with work. The ravages of the fall have often left us with frustration, disappointment, and futility in our work (as the Preacher says in Ecclesiastes 2:17–23). The farmer may work all year on his crop, only to have it all lost in a day from hail or locusts. The campus minister may work for two years training and mentoring and discipling a student leader, only to have them turn away from the faith. The pastor works faithfully to care for and nourish his flock, but some will fall away.

In spite of this, there are times when we love our work, when our work brings us great joy and blesses other people. The artist creates a masterpiece, the woodworker fashions a beautiful table, the surgeon resets the broken bone, the entrepreneur develops a thriving and useful business that provides a livelihood for many. When we use our God-given gifts and abilities to accomplish his work in this world, we are joyful, our life seems very full, and we are blessed.

The New Testament makes it very clear that we are to use our particular gifts to serve others. They are *gifts*, not entitlements. Applying the analogy of the human body, Paul speaks of the body of Christ, the church:

> For as in one body we have many members, and the members do not all have the same function, so we, though many, are one body in Christ, and individually members one of another. Having gifts that differ according to the grace given to us, let us use them. (Rom. 12:4–6)

Likewise, Peter reminds the church, "As each has received a gift, use it to serve one another, as good stewards of God's varied grace" (1 Pet. 4:10). Clearly, the immediate application for the use of these gifts is to serve the church in all its functions and callings. John Calvin, however, said these gifts ought to be exercised in the broader community as well. As we in the church extend our gifts — of serving, leading, administration, prayer, teaching, generosity, and healing — into the communities in which we live, we bless our neighbors and bring a powerful witness of the gospel to our neighborhood.

Without doubt, we experience the greatest joy in our work when we are serving within our "gift-set." I imagine that each of us has experienced the joy of zinging along when we are using our particular gifts for a good purpose, whether at home or in our job. It feels almost as though it took no effort at all. We may even be able to sit back and look at our work and say, "It is good. It is not perfect, but it is good." Perhaps we have also experienced the grind, like walking through deep mud, when we are operating outside our gifts. We may be expending a huge effort to accomplish seemingly very little.

Psychologist Mihaly Csikszentmihalyi has developed the idea of "living in flow" as a secret to happiness.[13] In studying athletes, he discovered that trained athletes often enter a state of complete absorption and focus on their sport or activity. It may be scaling a steep cliff, figure skating, or downhill skiing. In this state, they will lose all sense of time, place, surroundings, and even self-awareness. It may seem that the task has taken no time at all. They are doing what they know, what they are good at, and what they love. They are *in flow*.

This is also the case for highly skilled artists as they become engrossed in their painting or sculpture, or as musicians become absorbed in performing on the piano or violin. The same is true for the surgeon who enters the several-hour-long task of heart bypass surgery, or a dancer who becomes lost in their routine. Perhaps many of us have known this experience when we are performing a demanding task that we love for an extended time. It requires our full concentration, and we joyfully lose ourselves in it.

Indeed, it is important to figure out what we are good at, and what we are not good at, if we are to find joy in our work. It is equally important to seek a work situation where we can use our distinct gifts most effectively. This is not always easy. Many find themselves in jobs where their gifts are not being used very well. But they need to make a living, and so they endure until they can find a better fit. At the same time, we live in an imperfect world, and there is probably no job that will be a perfect fit for our gifts. Any job will require some tasks that do not match our gifts, and any job will fail to make use of other gifts that we do have. Someone once shared this simple diagram with a group of us InterVarsity leaders, and I have found it very helpful in counseling people about job fit:

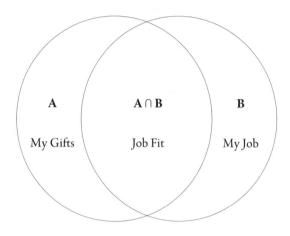

In this Venn diagram that compares "my job" and "my gifts," the A portion of the first circle represents gifts that I possess, but that the job does not require. I may need to find hobbies or volunteer work to use these extra gifts. The B portion of the second circle represents aspects that the job requires where my gifts are not strong. I will need to work harder to get these done or form partnerships with others to compensate for my lack of ability in this area. The intersecting portion of the circles (A∩B) is where my gifts and the job requirements match. This diagram suggests a pretty healthy job fit. But if the A section or the B section is much larger, then it is not a good job fit. I may be able to survive for a time in this kind of mismatched job, but ultimately, I should be looking for another job with a better fit for my gifts.

When we find our calling, our vocation, our life work, we can experience great joy in fulfilling that calling with the gifts God has given us. I have had various jobs and roles in my life, but they all point in some way to my calling to the students and faculty in the university world. This has been my heartthrob, my passion. Frederick Buechner said it so well: "The place God calls you to is the place where your deep gladness and the world's deep hunger meet."[14] When we find that place, we can joyfully pour ourselves into that work, without hesitation, without resentment, without feeling cheated. You may feel, as I often have, "I can't believe I get paid to do this." You may even find yourself whistling while you work.

Fruit That Will Last

And this work will bear fruit. In John 15:16 Jesus tells his disciples, "You did not choose me, but I chose you and appointed you that you should go and bear fruit and that your fruit should abide."

One of the joys of my reaching an advanced stage of life is that I have lived to see some long-term fruit of some of my labors. Brian and Rachel were students at Grand Valley State University in the 1980s, when it offered radically alternative educational programs. Brian had just become a Christian, but he wasn't sure exactly what that meant. I spent a year discipling him, meeting weekly for Bible study and discussion, and mostly talking about the pressing questions on his mind. One pressing question on his mind was a young woman student named Rachel. He was interested in her, but she was really into Eastern religions. Could I meet with her? We met, and she was surprisingly open. I asked if she would be willing to read C. S. Lewis's *Mere Christianity*. She did. We discussed it, and she was soon convinced and ready to become a Jesus follower. A year later, she was attending the Urbana Student Missions Conference. She said Brian was "talking marriage." What did I think?

I said I thought it sounded wonderful. They got married and went on to have seven children. Rachel did some homeschooling and is very active in the community. Brian is an entrepreneur and a businessman and is very active in numerous Christian ministries, especially those focused on the family.

There is joy in serving Jesus. Yes, there are disappointments and frustrations along the way. But when we are in a place where our gifts are being used, where people are being genuinely helped, where we can point people to Jesus, where we can pour ourselves into our work, but where we can leave the results to God — we can serve with joy and gratitude.

Thank you, Lord, for the privilege of serving in your name, under your gaze and your smile. Amen.

Reflection Questions

1. Do you find yourself wanting to protect your time and energies from being used up? This stands in contrast to Jesus's model of giving himself for others. What is the fear behind this tendency toward self-protectiveness?

2. The life of generosity is the joyful life. How might you take steps to becoming more generous toward others?

3. Do you have an understanding of your personal strengths, your spiritual gifts? Consider asking a trusted friend what they think are your gifts and special abilities.

4. Do you normally view others as persons, not problems? Do you see each person as made in the image of God, with value and dignity?

5. Have you found your life calling, that place where God can use your unique set of gifts for his service in this world?

10

Joy and Worship

Throughout human history, people have worshipped something — gods and goddesses; idols of gold, wood, and stone; the sun and the moon; ancestors; the spirits. In our secular age, this worship has shifted to human reason, science, technology, the arts, sex, and the endless diversions now available to us on the internet. We were made for worship. As humans, we will worship something. It is our nature.[1]

Men and women of the university, I see that in every way you are very religious. As I walked around the university, I observed carefully your objects of worship. I saw your altar called the stadium where many of you worship the sports deity. I saw the science building where many place their hope for the salvation of mankind. I found your altar to the fine arts where artistic expression and performance seem to reign supreme without subservience to any greater power. I walked through your residence halls and observed your sex goddess posters and evidence of kegger praise gatherings. Yet as I talked with some of you and saw the emptiness in your eyes and sensed the aching in your hearts, I perceived that in your heart is yet another altar, an altar to the Unknown God whom you suspect may be there. You have a sense that there is something more than these humanistic and self-indulgent gods. What you long for as something unknown, I want to declare to you now.

This is a portion of a paraphrase that came to me as I was ministering in the university world and studying the apostle Paul's visit to Athens in the first century (Acts 17:22–34). I later visited the site where he delivered his famous address before the Areopagus, and I delivered the same one. It was the off-season, so there was no one around to hear my eloquent speech. Just a lonely dog that barked and ran off. Since the Areopagus was an ancient university of sorts, I wondered how the great apostle might have responded if he had been placed in front of the faculty of a modern-day university. And so I wrote this paraphrase to try to capture the scene.

As Christians, we believe that worship is our highest calling, our greatest expression of faith, as we ascribe to the Lord the glory that is due his name (Ps. 29:1–2; 96:7–10). In doing so, we are lifted up to the highest level of what it means to be human. It is what we were made for. We will never do a more noble act than lifting our hearts to worship God in spirit and in truth. And therefore, worship is also our supreme joy. It is immensely liberating to express our joy in thanksgiving, praise, and adoration, with music and dancing, to the living God. "The joyful act of praising God — a thankfulness flowing almost automatically from recognition of God's gifts — is the central action of the human, the self-transcending act in which we begin to participate in our fullest flourishing."[2]

The Westminster Confession states that "the chief end of man is to glorify God and enjoy him forever." For believers, the worship of God, both personally and corporately, is our central purpose in life. As we worship, there is a sense in which we lose ourselves, and we are caught up in the glory of God. It is also our greatest joy. After all, we are to *enjoy* God forever, not just serve and obey him.

Worship is first of all a response to God's gracious invitation to come to him. More precisely, we come to him by the means he has established, whereby we may approach him and thus know his pleasure, his joy, and his blessing. The means of approaching God's throne is Jesus Christ our great high priest (Heb. 4:14–16). Worship is God-ordained, not man-made. Rather than making God into our own image, we want to worship him for who he is, not who we imagine him to be. We want to worship him in a manner that is worthy of his majesty and holiness.

> Ascribe to the LORD the glory due his name;
>> bring an offering and come into his courts!
> Worship the LORD in the splendor of holiness;
>> tremble before him, all the earth! (Ps. 96:8–9)

> Make a joyful noise to the LORD, all the earth;
>> break forth into joyous song and sing praises!
> Sing praises to the LORD with the lyre,
>> with the lyre and the sound of melody!
> With trumpets and the sound of the horn
>> make a joyful noise before the King, the LORD!
>> (Ps. 98:4–6)

> Enter his gates with thanksgiving,
>> and his courts with praise!
> Give thanks to him; bless his name! (Ps. 100:4)

Some of my greatest moments of joy come from worshipping regularly with God's people in my home church (and this being a Presbyterian church!). I am often struck by the thought, early in the time of worship, perhaps in a song, a prayer, or a word of Scripture — "Yes, this is the truth, this is what is real, this is what I believe deep down in my soul." I am moved by the music, touched by a prayer, exhorted by the Scripture, surprised again by the gospel, met by Christ at the Communion table. And once again, joy floods my heart.

There are many voices in our culture calling for our attention, with claims of what is important in life. We need to come aside often, with God's people, to give attention to God's voice, to be reminded of what is really real.

Blissful Worship

I remember being at an Urbana Student Missions Conference in the large arena at the University of Illinois with eighteen thousand students and missionaries, singing "All Hail the Power of Jesus' Name," with the rolling bass part and the floating soprano notes. "Crown him . . . crown him Lord of all." It just about knocked me over, and I thought to myself, "I will never be the same." It was life-changing. And I have never forgotten that moment. It is a joy that far surpasses any pleasure this world can offer.

Being a Reformed type myself, I am not easily given over to thoughts of ecstasy or mystical religious experiences. To be honest, many of us who call ourselves Reformed evangelicals often operate as functional naturalists.[3] We have disavowed the more spectacular spiritual gifts. We don't really expect to see the supernatural breaking into our lives. But if God is real, and as our hearts are open, we would expect to sometimes weep in prayer, to tremble at his voice, and to shiver with delight when an old truth comes with fresh impact. The Spirit blows where he will. When we worship the transcendent God, we would expect to experience something beyond the ordinariness of life. As we encounter the beauty and goodness of God, we may be lifted out of the natural realm and into the divine. Joy is a response to that which lifts us beyond our common imaginings. "Joy speaks immediately of transcendence, of what is outside."[4]

"What no eye has seen, nor ear heard,
  nor the heart of man imagined,
 what God has prepared for those who love him."
(1 Cor. 2:9)

Ecstasy, excessive rapture, should not be confined to the more charismatic styles of worship. Why should they have all the fun! *Ekstasis* suggests moving out of our staid position, moving out of our comfort zone, into the unknown, into deep communion with God and our neighbor.[5] Surely worship is to be a blissful, even ecstatic experience for all who fully enter in spirit and in truth. It is often said that Reformed folks are very good at the "truth" aspect but not so great in the "spirit," whereas charismatics are very strong in the "spirit" but not always so attentive to the "truth." But Jesus made it clear that "the true worshipers will worship the Father in spirit *and* truth, for the Father is seeking such people to worship him" (John 4:23).

This dual aspect of worship is what David Bentley Hart calls "bliss" in his book *The Experience of God: Being, Consciousness, and Bliss.*[6] Besides being a devastating critique of naturalism, this book is a bold assertion of the validity of our experience with God. To say that I have touched the heart of God in prayer is a valid truth claim. Bliss is our instinctive response to the good, the beautiful, and the true — that which transcends the natural order and rescues us from our preoccupation with our autonomous, individualistic selves.

Becoming like What We Worship

There is also a mystery about worship — that is, that we tend to become like that which we truly worship, that which we most revere. The prophet Isaiah launches an extended diatribe against the falseness and futility of worshipping idols (Isa. 41–45). He declares pagan idols to be lies, empty, shameful, and worse than nothing.

Those who worship them will be put to shame. But the truth and consequences of idolatry are even more immediate. The psalmist reminds us that those who make such idols and those who trust in them will become like them.

> The idols of the nations are silver and gold,
>   made by human hands.
> They have mouths, but cannot speak,
>   eyes, but cannot see.
> They have ears, but cannot hear,
>   nor is there breath in their mouths.
> Those who make them will be like them,
>   and so will all who trust in them.
>   (Ps. 135:15–18; cf. 115:4–8)

"We resemble what we revere, either for ruin or restoration."[7] When we worship idols that can neither hear nor see nor speak, we ourselves become dull of hearing, spiritually blind, speaking falsehood. If we worship money, sex, and power — the three great temptations of our day — we will always crave more; we will become shallow, empty, fearful, dirty, insecure, dissatisfied, and disillusioned. The fact is that worshipping anything else but the one true God will eventually eat you alive. Consider the devastating results delineated in Romans 1 as a result of idolatry.

> Although they claimed to be wise, they became fools and exchanged the glory of the immortal God for images made to look like a mortal human being and birds and animals and reptiles. (Rom. 1:22–23)

On the other hand, the wonderful, joyful truth about worshipping God is that, through Christ, as we gaze into his lovely face, contemplating his glory, we are increasingly becoming transformed into *his* glory. This is one of the surprising benefits of true worship. This is the place where we feel most content, satisfied, cleansed, filled up, and at peace — the place where we are molded more and more into Christ's image. Paul states this truth clearly:

> And we all, who with unveiled faces contemplate the Lord's glory, are being transformed into his image with ever-increasing glory, which comes from the Lord, who is the Spirit. (2 Cor. 3:18)

We are all being transformed, whether we realize it or not, in one direction or another. We are either moving further from God or toward him. We are either becoming more like the false and empty gods we worship, or we are being amazingly transformed into the very image of Christ.

The Power of Joy in Worship

Joyful worship is powerful. Ezra the priest said to the exiles after their return to Jerusalem, "Do not be grieved, the joy of the LORD is your strength" (Neh. 8:10). It was a surprising statement in the context. Ezra was preaching; that is, he was reading from the book of the Law and giving its meaning, for many hours. The people of God were hearing the reading of the Law, some for the very first time. As they listened, the people wept, perhaps in realizing how much they had lost while in exile, how far from God's laws they had strayed. And as they listened, the leaders realized that this very day was in fact a holy day, the Festival of Tabernacles. And the Old Testament festivals were times of joy and celebration. And so the leaders instructed the people to stop their weeping and lamenting because they were required to rejoice and celebrate on this day (cf. Lev. 23:40–41).

When we enter into genuine, heartfelt worship and praise to God, our spirits are lifted, our strength is renewed, we sense the Lord's presence, his face upon us. We encounter the Lord's great joy, and our hearts swell, and his joy lightens our day. Jürgen Moltmann speaks of "the *great joy* in the *broad place* of God who is nearer to us than we believe and enlarging our life more than we think":

> Joy is the power to live, to love, to have creative initiative. Joy awakens all our senses, energizing mind and body. How do we experience this power in the presence of the "living God" (Pss. 42:2; 84:2)? How is our life resonating the immense joy of God?[8]

The face of God, or the countenance of God upon us, is the sign of his blessing and gives us great joy. The psalmist speaks often of the Lord's face upon us, and other times when God hides his face. We see it also in the Aaronic benediction:

> The LORD bless you and keep you;
> the LORD make his face to shine upon you and be
> gracious to you;
> the LORD lift up his countenance upon you and give
> you peace. (Num. 6:24–26)

Have you ever found yourself outside, basking in the sun, soaking up its blessed light and warmth, noticing how it illuminates the trees, the water, and the earth? Life is good. You have joy and peace. Then suddenly the sun is gone. Perhaps a cloud has blocked its shine, or perhaps it has descended beneath the mountain ridge. You feel a tinge of sadness, disappointment, loss. This captures in a very small way the mood of the psalmist: "Then you hid your face, and I was dismayed" (Ps. 30:7). God's blessed gaze upon us is much more significant than the sun's rays. When we sense God's pleasure, his joy, upon us, we are filled with joy, and once again, "the joy of the LORD is your strength."

Yes, the joy of the Lord is our strength, and when we lose it, we feel weak and dragged down, with sagging spirits, sapped strength. Joy is closely associated with courage, just as joylessness is connected to weakness (Acts 27:22). It is in obedience, faith, trust, and a sense of our complete dependence on the Lord that we know his blessed presence and blessed countenance. And it is in repentance that we can be restored to joyful communion with God once again (see chapter 6).

Any theology of joy must be a church theology. It is the church that is well positioned and equipped to cultivate joy in the lives of God's people, and any who would enter in. In the Christian community we learn how to understand the story of our lives within God's sovereign work in history and redemption. The word and sacraments help us to reenact the central truths of God's gracious activity in the world and in our lives.[9]

As we worship, particularly as we worship together with the saints, we especially sense God's pleasure and joy over us. It was the regular practice of the early church to "devote themselves to the apostles' teaching and the fellowship, to the breaking of bread and the prayers" (Acts 2:42). The psalmist longs for, yearns for, the "courts of the LORD." He can't wait to return and enter into that blissful worship of God once again.

> My soul longs, yes, faints
>   for the courts of the LORD;
> my heart and flesh sing for joy
>   to the living God
> . . . .

For a day in your courts is better
than a thousand elsewhere.
I would rather be a doorkeeper in the house of my God
than dwell in the tents of wickedness. (Ps. 84:2, 10)

Worship as Witness

Worship is also a powerful witness to those outside the church, as they observe the saints caught up in their dance of love for the Lord. As we lose ourselves and allow ourselves to be lifted up into the Lord's presence, something wonderful happens. On the occasions where even skeptics have opportunity to witness this genuine worship of God, they take notice, and they are drawn to this experience.

Over thirty-five years of ministering among university students at camps and conferences, I have seen this happen again and again. Frequently, Christian students will invite their nonbelieving friends to come with them to these events. And as they watch these believers in worship, it is a new experience for them. They are dumbstruck. For some, it is the first time they have encountered Christian worship. For many, it is the key that opens their hearts to consider the reality of the claims of Christian faith. They find themselves drawn, longing for this kind of experience, to be lifted beyond themselves to a much larger, transcendent God.

Having followed the music of Bob Dylan since the 1960s, I tracked with great interest his conversion to the Christian faith in 1979 and the three years of Christian concerts that followed, concerts that were laced with preaching and testimony (much to the chagrin of his devoted fans). Dylan endured a good deal of jeering, insults, and food throwing while onstage. As the people shouted, "Just sing rock and roll!," he responded, "You want rock and roll?

Let me tell you about the Rock. It is Jesus Christ, and he is the way, the truth, and the life."

But mostly, these concerts were times of worship, with Dylan and his entourage, the band and Black gospel singers, expressing their praise and adoration to God. Many music critics were clearly puzzled, trying to figure out what happened to their hero. In fact, Dylan expert and music journalist Paul Williams wrote a book in 1980, *Dylan — What Happened?*, to try to deal with the question everyone was asking. As Williams attended concert after concert, he sometimes watched this group onstage as they worshipped God with such sincerity and genuine emotion and found himself wishing he could enter into that experience of worship. Later, commenting on Dylan's lyric "Surrender your crown on this blood-stained ground, take off your mask," Williams said, "It is one of the most powerful lines Dylan has ever written. And I won't argue with the fact that, now that the mask is off, the naked man underneath is more beautiful than ever, because the glory of God shines through him."[10]

The dominant theme in Dylan's gospel songs is gratitude, as in his 1980 song "What Can I Do for You?" "You have given everything to me," the song says. "What can I do for You?" This line alternates throughout with a list of things for which Dylan is eternally thankful: "You have laid down Your life for me / What can I do for You?"

Israel's Finest Hour

To me, one of the most moving moments of Old Testament worship comes with the construction of the tabernacle. It was a time when all of Israel came together with their offerings, their material resources, and their talents to complete this place of worship. God had instructed Moses about the details of the project, and Moses gathered the people together.

Moses said to all the congregation of the people of Israel, "This is the thing that the LORD has commanded. Take from among you a contribution to the LORD. Whoever is of a generous heart, let him bring the LORD's contribution: gold, silver, and bronze; blue and purple and scarlet yarns and fine twined linen; goats' hair, tanned rams' skins, and goatskins; acacia wood, oil for the light, spices for the anointing oil and for the fragrant incense, and onyx stones and stones for setting, for the ephod and for the breastpiece. Let every skillful craftsman among you come and make all that the LORD has commanded." (Exod. 35:4–10)

Then the people returned to their homes. As the Lord moved in their hearts, they began to gather their gold, silver, bronze, precious stones, leather, fine yarn, oils and spices. They used their skills to craft wool and linens. Then they brought it all to Moses as a freewill offering to the Lord. Wave upon wave of people kept coming with more gifts, until Moses finally had to say, "No more. We have more than enough to complete the work" (Exod. 36:6–7).

What a testimony of the Lord's blessing. When God's Spirit is in the hearts of the people, there is no need for begging and coercing to gather the money and resources needed. This story would surely be the envy of any church building program today. I have known some cases where this kind of generosity was expressed by a congregation, and the people gave over and above what was needed, but it is rare. When giving is understood as an expression of worship, and the people's hearts are open to the Lord's leading, then God's people are moved to give generously and joyfully (2 Cor. 9:6–8).

Now what was needed was someone to lead this tabernacle project. The Lord chose Bezalel to be the chief architect of the tabernacle and chief craftsman of all its furnishings, along with Oholiab. They were to guide the process and train others in the work.

[The LORD] has filled him with the Spirit of God, with skill, with intelligence, with knowledge, and with all craftsmanship, to devise artistic designs, to work in gold and silver and bronze, in cutting stones for setting, and in carving wood, for work in every skilled craft. . . . He has filled them with skill to do every sort of work done by an engraver or by a designer or by an embroiderer in blue and purple and scarlet yarns and fine twined linen, or by a weaver — by any sort of workman or skilled designer. (Exod. 35:31–33, 35)

A friend of mine who is an artist told me that this list includes such a variety of artistic specialties that it would extend to six different departments in a present-day college of art.

Bezalel is not someone who is often mentioned as one of the heroes of faith. But this was his finest hour and in many ways the culmination of his life's work. His heart must have burst with joy that his gifts and skills were being recognized, and that he was chosen for this magnificent task. He must have also been very frightened by the enormity and the sanctity of the project.

So, as I am sometimes prone to do, I began to imagine what went on in the mind of Bezalel as he took on this daunting commission. Let's listen to his thoughts:

Bezalel — that's the name that was given to me by my father Uri, my grandfather Hur. It means "in the shadow of God." I could use some of God's shadow now. I am of the tribe of Judah and my trade is master craftsman, which up to now has been an enjoyable, fulfilling life. I've always seemed to have some skill in using my hands, ever since I was a boy. Just give me some wood, precious stones, gold, silver, bronze, cloth, and I can shape them into something beautiful, even magnificent. The work is hard, but it's what I love to do. Many of the people of Israel carry and treasure my artistic works.

Chapter 10

But now Moses says God has chosen me to lead this project of building the tabernacle, the sanctuary of God. What man could be up to such a task? It's beyond any human means. I thought, "Where will we get the laborers?" But then all the most skilled people of our community began coming to me and volunteering for service. I said to Moses, "Where will we ever get the materials — the gold, silver, precious stones, fine cloth, and wood — for such a project?" But then the people began coming forward with offerings, day after day, and soon we had more than enough materials to complete the task. We had to tell Moses to order the people to stop bringing their offerings. I wept at their generosity and their trust.

I began to realize that the Lord was behind this project in a unique way. But it was a small comfort, because now everyone was looking to me to orchestrate the building of this dwelling place for God Almighty. That is my dilemma. How can a man ever design and craft something adequate enough, something suitable as a dwelling place for the Creator God? I tremble at the thought of making anything that would insult the Lord's holiness and majesty.

Moses says, "Make the ark of the covenant. Make a cover for the ark, a cover of mercy and atonement, with two cherubim facing each other, with their wings spread so as to overshadow and protect the ark." I cried out to God, "How can a man design such a thing? What do cherubim look like?" No answer.

But it's strange — as I began to put my hands to the task, God's Spirit seemed to come over me in such a manner that I knew, I knew what it should look like. And as I began working with the other craftsmen on the various aspects of the project, we all had a sense that what was being built was somehow beyond us. The project seemed to take on a direction of its own. We were both participants and witnesses at the same time. When it was finished, there was a magnificence and majesty about it that was almost eerie.

But the culmination came when, after Moses had put everything in place and we all gathered round to consecrate it, the Cloud covered the tabernacle and the glory of the Lord filled the place. We fell back in awe. That was when I knew God was pleased with what we had built. Imagine that something crafted

by human hands, guided by God's Spirit, could receive God's approval in such
a dramatic way. I still tremble when I think of it.

It is pure joy when we give of our whole selves in worship and
service, when we truly encounter the almighty God. It has to make
us tremble at times. How could humble creatures like us be included
in such a divine communion? It is astonishing and wonderful.

Reflection Questions

1. Have you discovered joy in worship lately? Do you agree that worship is our highest calling, the greatest expression of our faith?
2. Do your corporate times of worship serve to remind you of what
   is true, what is real, in a world where many voices are calling for
   your attention?
3. We become like that which we worship. As we gaze upon the
   Lord Jesus in worship, we are being more and more transformed
   into his image. Try saying a little prayer the next time you enter
   your church worship time — Lord, as I worship you this morning, make me more like you.
4. Our work can also be worship. Are you aware of God's gaze
   upon you as you work or study? How can you offer your work
   as a gift pleasing to God?

II

Joy to the World

As a Protestant, I have been watching the life of Pope Francis with much interest and admiration. He travels the world and mingles with people, he sits with and prays with the sick and the dying, the poor, the disabled, the so-called untouchables. He emanates joy that is contagious, winsome, compassionate, and real. When you look at his face, it makes you want to smile.

Then I read his book *The Joy of the Gospel*[1] and discovered a man who is profoundly joyful about the power of the gospel, the good news of salvation. He is bold and unapologetic about the importance and relevance of this message for our world. It is a life-changing message that our world desperately needs to hear, and it speaks to people's deepest needs. We are reminded of Augustine's prayer: "Thou hast made us for thyself, O Lord, and our heart is restless until it finds its rest in thee."

This is a joy that must be shared. Francis speaks of dour Christians "whose lives seem like Lent without Easter" (8), which of course is reminiscent of the Narnia phrase "Always winter but never Christmas." Francis reminds us that Jesus is the first and greatest evangelist and that we must not lose heart, because our mission in this world is a continuation of his mission (13).

Sometimes we lose our enthusiasm for mission because we forget that the gospel responds to our deepest needs, since we were created for what the Gospel offers us. . . . If we succeed in expressing adequately and with beauty the essential content of the Gospel, surely this message will speak to the deepest yearnings of people's hearts. . . . Our infinite sadness can only be cured by infinite love. (178–79)

The pope admonishes his priests to evangelize their congregations. And in doing this, they must make better use of the homily to preach the gospel. With surprising humor, he uncovers the reality that the homily is often a cause of distress, both for clergy and for parishioner.

The homily is the touchstone for judging a pastor's closeness and ability to communicate with his people. We know that the faithful attach great importance to it, and that both they and the ordained ministers suffer because of homilies, the laity from having to listen to them and the clergy from having to preach them! (98)

He then proceeds to delineate for them an impressive mini-course in how to prepare and deliver an effective, biblically based, gospel-centered homily, concluding, "Let us renew our confidence in preaching" (98). Indeed, what a great gift this would be to the church.

Joy is something we must share with the world. The joy of God in our lives may be the most convincing apologetic for Christian faith in our day.[2] A life of joy, even in hardship, is a powerful and attractive testimony of God's grace in our lives. As I listen to people's testimonies of how they came to faith in Jesus, they will often say, "There was something about this Christian friend, a deep joy in her life, and I wanted to know the secret of that joy." Of course, it is not the expression of Christian joy that saves anyone, but that joy can open hearts to the one who can truly save them. This was my own experience, as I came into a small country church in Illinois where people really knew God and had the joy of the Lord. It was very attractive, and I found myself drawn to them, wanting to spend time with them. This allowed me to be open to dealing with the serious questions and doubts I had about Christian faith, and ultimately to embrace this faith as my own.

> We want our neighbors to see, feel, and experience the joy of God. . . . We want people to know just how amazingly the joy of God transforms every aspect of human life for those who receive it . . . to know that God is for them and not against them.[3]

Too often, the Christian message has appeared to be negative, where we seem more interested in forcing our moral values on society rather than demonstrating the joy of the gospel in action. If we hope to see the world receptive to the good news of Christ, we must convince them of our great desire for their better welfare. We must lead with love instead of what may appear to be a narrow political agenda. Issues such as abortion and gay marriage are extremely important, but the Christian faith is first of all a saving relationship with God, and morality flows from the transformation that emerges from that grand redemption. Our society is very aware of what evangelical Christians are *against*. They need to hear more about what we are *for*.[4] If people reject God's good news, let it be because of their pride, self-righteousness, and illusions of self-reliance, rather than because the good news is shrouded in a public morality they find offensive.

Joy to the World

Joy at Jesus's Coming

Joy to the world, the Lord is come!
Let earth receive her King;
let ev'ry heart prepare him room
and heav'n and nature sing,
and heav'n and nature sing,
and heav'n, and heav'n and nature sing.

Joy to the earth, the Savior reigns!
Let men their songs employ,
while fields and floods, rocks, hills, and plains
repeat the sounding joy,
repeat the sounding joy,
repeat, repeat the sounding joy.

No more let sins and sorrows grow,
nor thorns infest the ground;
he comes to make his blessings flow
far as the curse is found,
far as the curse is found,
far as, far as the curse is found.

He rules the world with truth and grace
and makes the nations prove
the glories of his righteousness
and wonders of his love,
and wonders of his love,
and wonders, wonders of his love.[5]

This popular Christmas carol by Isaac Watts — the most published carol in North America — makes some very bold claims. First, it makes an offer of "joy to the world." As we have seen, the advent of Jesus was marked by joy from beginning to end. "Fear not, for behold, I bring you good news of great joy that will be for all the people. For unto you is born this day in the city of David a Savior, who is Christ the Lord" (Luke 2:10–11). It is clear that something new is happening. The Savior, the Lord, the Messiah-King has arrived in the world with a message of joy, and this is good news indeed.

The second bold claim is that he comes to reign — not as a political ruler, and certainly not by force, but in the hearts of those who will receive him. "Let every heart prepare him room." His rule is like no other, characterized by "truth and grace" (see John 1:14). As Savior, he offers to forgive our sins, to deliver us from the bondage of self-indulgence and from the oppression of our self-centered lives. The reach of his salvation extends "far as the curse is found" — that is, to the very ends of our broken, fallen, and suffering world. In place of sin and sorrow, he brings healing and newness of life. As Lord, he invites us to follow him in a life of sacrificial love and in giving ourselves to others. As King, he invites us into his new kind of kingdom, marked by humility, meekness, righteousness, mercy, and peace (Matt. 5:1–16). This is why his coming changes everything, and this is why it is such joyfully good news.

As Alexander Schmemann famously asserts, Jesus came for the life of the world.[6] Jesus also died for the life of the world. Why would he do that? Because the Father loves this world (John 3:16), and in obedience to the Father, Jesus came to offer his life for the world. As Creator, this world and all who are in it belong to him (Psalm 24:1). And Jesus came to restore true life to this wayward world. As the Good Shepherd, Jesus announced, "I came that they might have life, and have it abundantly" (John 10:10). Jesus intends for his followers to have flourishing lives, overflowing with joy and blessing, to dwell securely in his care.[7]

Wake-Up Call

Imagine a child sitting on a beautiful beach, with the ocean spray sparkling, a gorgeous sunset unfolding, and the fishing boats returning for the night. But the child is staring at his cell phone, lost in a game and missing the whole scene. The father gently shakes him and says, "Son, you are missing something really important, something real and alive. Please wake up and turn your gaze from the phone and see the spectacular beauty before your eyes."

Jesus came as the light of the world to open the eyes of the physically and spiritually blind, that they might *see* the world as it truly is (John 9). He came to lovingly shake us awake from our illusions and slumber. Paul quotes an early Christian hymn to make this point:

> "Awake, O sleeper,
>   and arise from the dead,
>   and Christ will shine on you." (Eph. 5:14)

And again Paul says, "The hour has come for you to wake from sleep. For salvation is nearer to us now than when we first believed" (Rom. 13:11). Many in our world are living in a dream, under a spell. Many of us have lost sight of the fullness of life God intends for us — lost in trivial pursuits, indulgent vices, petty ambitions, and escapist hobbies.

C. S. Lewis comments on the importance of breaking this spell:

Do you think I am trying to weave a spell? Perhaps I am; but remember your fairy tales. Spells are used for breaking enchantments as well as for inducing them. And you and I have need of the strongest spell that can be found to wake us from the evil enchantment of worldliness which has been laid upon us for nearly a hundred years. Almost our whole education has been directed to silencing this shy, persistent, inner voice; almost all our modern philosophies have been devised to convince us that the good of man is to be found on this earth.[8]

Keith Green wrote of his own conversion as a Jesus follower in terms of waking up from a long dream:

> Like waking up from the longest dream, how real it
> seemed
> Until your love broke through
> I've been lost in a fantasy, that blinded me
> Until your love broke through.[9]

The light of Jesus helps us to see things as they really are. It allows us to see ourselves truly and clearly, as people made in God's image who have lost our way. And we can see the world for what it is: a holy and sacred creation of God that has also lost its way. This world is a dark place, but the light of Jesus is able to dispel the darkness and show us the truth.

We live in a day when the internet offers nonstop diversions. We can immerse ourselves endlessly in a virtual world of everything from games, news, porn, movies, chats, photos, and stories. Meanwhile, the real world is passing us by. There is a deadening effect in these diversions, even worthy diversions, that keeps us from seeing the world truly and from seeing ourselves as made in God's image, made for relationship with God and other people.

Jesus claimed to be the light of the world. He used the image of light to convey the idea of truth or reality:

The light shines in the darkness, and the darkness has not overcome it. (John 1:5)

The true light, which gives light to everyone, was coming into the world. (John 1:8)

"I have come into the world as light, so that whoever believes in me may not remain in darkness." (John 12:46)

This brings us to the larger question: What was Jesus's mission in this world? John's Gospel records several "I am" statements by Jesus that help us discern an answer. These include "I am the bread of life," "I am the light of the world," "I am the good shepherd," "I am the resurrection and the life," "I am the way, the truth, and the life," and "I am the true vine." Together, these statements point to Jesus's power and authority, his divinity, and his all-sufficiency as our life source.

Jesus's Mission in the World

Jesus did not come to earth merely as a reformer, or simply to show us a new way to live. In his earthly ministry, he did indeed reveal a whole new way of life, and a new kingdom, and this was a necessary and vital part of his mission. But it would be a mistake to think that Jesus could have accomplished his radical mission in this world only by providing a new model for living. We were not just in need of a new philosophy to straighten out our misguided thinking. The condition of our world and of our own hearts was much graver than that. This world needed a full, transformative redemption. We needed supernatural reconciliation with God in order to have reconciliation with one another. And this could be accomplished only by a sacrifice — the perfect, innocent, voluntary offering of the Son of God for us (Eph. 5:2).

It is no happenstance that the Gospel accounts spend an inordinate amount of space detailing that last week of Jesus's life. In Matthew, Mark, and Luke, about one-third of the pages are devoted to that final week. In John's Gospel, it is close to one-half. From the beginning it was clear that Jesus came as a Savior to offer his life as a sacrifice, the ultimate Passover lamb, for the sins of the world (1 Cor. 5:7). From the cryptic prophetic words of Simeon to Mary in the temple at Jesus's presentation as an infant ("a sword will pierce through your own soul also," Luke 2:35) to the heralding proclamation of John the Baptist ("Behold the lamb of God who takes away the sin of the world," John 1:29), the mission of Jesus's coming as an offering for sin is made clear. In addition, Jesus clearly explained to his disciples that he must go to Jerusalem to suffer at the hands of the chief priests and be killed, and then to rise again the third day (Matt. 16:21; Mark 8:31; Luke 24:44–47).

Without the atoning work of Christ on the cross, there could not have been real joy to the world. There could not be peace on earth, or goodwill to all people, or justice for the poor and oppressed. But the good news of the gospel is that "Christ died for our sins in accordance with the Scriptures, that he was buried, that he was raised on the third day in accordance with the Scriptures" (1 Cor. 15:3–4). It is this gospel that has the power to transform us, because it is the "power of God for salvation to everyone who believes" (Rom. 1:16).

Every year we celebrate Palm Sunday, with the waving of palms, the singing of hosannas. It is a joyful, triumphant occasion. The King is coming — lay your palms and your garments in the road for him! The children are jubilant. As Frederick Buechner suggests, perhaps there is a part of us that wishes maybe this time it will be different. This time Pilate will relent. This time the crowd will shout for Jesus to be released instead of Barabbas, Judas will not betray him, the chief priests will open their hearts to him.[10] This time he won't have to die. But it is to no avail. There is no escaping the cross — not for Jesus, not for us. The Passover lamb must be offered once for all, for the sins of the world. And our ultimate joy is not on Palm Sunday but on Easter Sunday, when redemption has been accomplished and the Lord is risen indeed.

Yes, Jesus lived in this world. He revealed who he was: the Messiah, the Son of God (Matt. 16:15–17). His miracles substantiated his claims. He made known his authority over every sphere of life. He revealed God to us (Heb. 1:1–3). He ministered to people in their weakness, poverty, sickness, and even death. He brought good news to the poor, liberty to the captives, and sight to the blind (Luke 4:18–19). His earthly ministry had three components: he healed people, he proclaimed the gospel of the kingdom, and he defeated the spiritual forces of darkness (Matt. 9:35–38). In so doing, Jesus brought bursts of joy into people's lives, people like Mary Magdalene (Luke 8:2–3), the madman in chains (Mark 5:1–20), the Samaritan woman (John 4), Zacchaeus (Luke 19:1–10), and Nicodemus (John 3). Their lives were forever transformed.

But all the while, he set his face toward Jerusalem (Luke 9:51), where he had to suffer and die so that these same people could have final transformation and eternal life to live with him forever (John 11:25).

Obstacles to Joy

As C. S. Lewis declared, the world into which Jesus came was "enemy-occupied territory." "Christianity is the story of how the rightful king has landed, you might say landed in disguise, and is calling us all to take part in a great campaign of sabotage."[11] While many did receive Jesus and his joyful message of the kingdom of heaven, many others did not, especially the religious leaders and the power structure of Rome, who were threatened by him for different reasons. John summarizes the incongruity of it all: "He was in the world, and the world was made by him, but the world did not know him" (John 1:10). The world that God created is fallen, broken, and in rebellion. People are prone to assert their own wills and autonomy instead of accepting a trusting relationship with the God who made them.

And for us today, in trying to bring God's gift of joy into our modern world, we quickly bump into some serious obstacles. It should be obvious by now that our greatest joys stem from that which we love — our encounters with beauty, our ability to be astonished, the discovery of new truth, the worship of God, our deepest friendships, and the experience of gratitude. But we find ourselves in a secularized, largely materialist world that strikes at the core of each of these greatest joys. This world has little interest in God or religion or transcendence (anything beyond the natural realm, or even our own flesh). With the abandonment of transcendence, we have lost ultimate meaning and purpose and the basis for virtue, and all of life has been reduced to material, mechanical processes. Our present existence is attributed to a cosmic quirk. Some materialists would suggest we have evolved to this level where we now happen to have the illusion of consciousness, the idea of possessing a mind or a soul. But apparently, it is all a cruel joke resulting from our present stage in evolutionary development. In our secular age, the idea of the divine and the supernatural is either ignored altogether or relegated to the furthest margins of social consciousness and public life.

1. The Great Disenchantment: Our Secular Age

Now I am going to take a more academic approach than I have so far in this book. So feel free to skip over this section if you wish. But I feel compelled to attempt to delve into the underlying causes of skepticism about religion and God and the supernatural in our modern Western world, the belief that God is an outdated idea in the age of science.

The Enlightenment of the seventeenth century ushered in the age of reason and the explosion of science, and has contributed greatly to our understanding of how the world works. Along with these advances in science and technology came the demystifying of many of the mysteries of the universe and the casting off of the shackles of ignorance and superstition. With that came the rise of humanism, an unbounded confidence in human achievement, a new sense of power and control over the world and of our ability to solve what was perceived as the remaining "few" impediments to human progress and self-actualization.

The Enlightenment places the autonomous, individual *self* squarely at the center of the universe. Children of the Enlightenment, at least in the West, are social "orphans." They no longer define themselves by their family heritage, their community, or their "place" (to borrow a concept from Wendell Berry), but rather as free agents. Each person is to find their own way in an increasingly pluralistic society. In *The Seven Storey Mountain*, Thomas Merton describes his own conversion to faith. After reading William Blake, Merton says he became convicted of "the dark and selfish rationalism which had been freezing my mind and will."[12]

With this new understanding, we find ourselves in a disenchanted world, a secular world, with the loss of transcendence, of miracles and the supernatural, of the sacred, and of the important role of the imagination. It is a world where scientific knowledge is more highly valued than religious belief. It becomes very difficult to find agreed-upon moral values, or a common good, other than the current reigning majority opinion.

This disenchantment is examined in depth, and critiqued, by philosopher Charles Taylor in his nine-hundred-page volume *A Secular Age*.[13] Taylor summarizes his goal this way: "The change I want to define and trace is one which takes us from a society in which it was virtually impossible not to believe in God, to one in which faith, even for the staunchest believer, is one human possibility among others."[14] Taylor traces this massive cultural transition back to not just the Enlightenment and the age of reason, but the Reformation, and especially Calvinism, with its disciplined and rational view of the world and strong view of human achievement.[15] This gradually led to the rise of Deism, the belief in a Creator God who essentially wound up the world and set it on its own course. Many of our American founding fathers were enamored with Deism and ruled out the possibility of divine revelation in favor of rational thinking and observation of nature as the sufficient source of all truth, including religious belief.

The rise of secularism is also scrutinized in the writings of sociologists Max Weber and Peter Berger. Berger describes how the new ruling plausibility structure evolved from the assumption of the supernatural to the dominance of the secular or the physical world.[16] Weber writes, "The fate of our times is characterized by rationalization and intellectualization and, above all, by the disenchantment (German: *Entzauberung*) of the world." But the world remains a "great enchanted garden." This is not to suggest that the medieval perception was one filled with "magical thinking" about the world, but that it was one that acknowledged the supernatural and a place of ultimate cause.[17]

C. S. Lewis, in *The Abolition of Man*, laments this loss, which he contends is now built into our educational system.[18] The focus on science, rationalism, and technology, the loss of a classical education, and the new subjectivity produce what Lewis calls "men without chests" — that is, people without imagination, virtue, intuition, and a sense of wonder, who are unable to grasp the most important elements of our humanity, like love, longing, beauty, ecstasy, humor, loyalty, and intuitive thinking. Lewis speaks of this loss in his own life. For Lewis, reading George MacDonald's fairy stories "baptized his imagination" and awoke in him an awareness of the transcendent. MacDonald and others believed that the imagination was an important aid in the search for and discovery of truth. By "imagination," we do not mean fanciful ideas. The master scientist uses imagination when they consider various possible explanations for a new discovery. In this sense, it is very close to the idea of intuition, which is essential to the progress of science. The devaluing of imagination is a serious problem in our culture. Our imagination is essential to experiencing the fullness of life. It is also essential to the experience of Christian faith.

What does all this have to do with the experience of joy? Everything! The disenchanted state of our world stultifies many of our greatest sources of joy.

2. *A Crisis of Meaning: Is That All There Is?*

It is not universal, but the predominant scientific mindset in our day continues to view all of life as deriving from purely mechanical, chemical processes. When taken to its logical extent, this worldview results in a crisis of meaning and the demise of joy. I am not at all suggesting that the work of science and the experience of joy are at odds with each other. Can a scientist who loves truth experience joy? Of course, but because she *loves* truth and believes she may be discovering some new secret that is really there in the universe, a discovery that matters, perhaps something that will serve the well-being of humanity. And if the scientist is operating from a Christian worldview, they will also know ecstatic joy and gratitude for the breathtakingly wonderful gift of creation God has endowed upon us. However, if the scientist operates with the prevailing view that all of life's processes must be explained merely by physical and chemical forces and modes of operation, and if this viewpoint is self-consciously held, then they must conclude that life is absurd. This will surely suck all the meaning and wonder out of life, all that makes life worth living, and with it the joy.

I realize that some will make heroic attempts to establish their own meaning in life. After all, we must latch onto something in order to keep on keeping on, and to make life seem worth living. Many others simply lose themselves in a multitude of distractions and amusements — anything to soothe the ache of hopelessness and meaninglessness, to avoid the implications of a life without God and without intrinsic purpose.

> But such avoidance will never make us happy. In fact, such an approach ends up making all of our pleasures hollow, for they serve as only momentary pauses in the endless drama of manipulation we play with the world. Experience becomes wholly a matter of evasion, of avoiding the facts of our life, of escape, a way of staving off the emptiness of our lives.[19]

In our more honest moments of reflection, it would seem we are left with the message of the popular 1960s song sung by Peggy Lee. After enumerating her experiences with life's great disappointments, she concludes,

Is that all there is?
If that's all there is, my friends, then let's keep dancing
Let's break out the booze and have a ball.[20]

Many people find a level of meaning and purpose by attaching themselves to some higher human cause or movement. Soldiers often return from battle missing the level of brotherhood they experienced on the front lines. But these experiences are short-lived unless they are rooted in some larger, transcendent purpose, a purpose that existed before us and will continue to exist after us. Apart from this, after all is said and done, we are left with the conclusion, "Let us therefore eat, drink, and be merry, for tomorrow we die." And that is all there is.

3. Finding Meaning in the Natural World

The Hungarian-born British physical chemist and philosopher Michael Polanyi argues very convincingly that the natural world reveals a propensity toward meaning at every level.[21] The movement from inanimate objects to the living organism, and the development of the DNA molecule from the simplest organism to human DNA, reveals a movement toward meaning, toward the achievement of a purpose, a telos.

> Moreover, looking at the general direction the evolutionary development of living organisms has taken, one must in all fairness admit that this direction has been toward more meaningful organizations — more meaningful in terms of their structure and in terms of the meanings they are able to achieve. . . .
>
> We are thus able to think that real discovery in science is possible for us because we are guided by an intuition of a more

meaningful organization of our knowledge of nature provided by the slope of deepening meaning in the whole field of potential meaning surrounding us. . . . We might justifiably claim, therefore, that everything we know is full of meaning, is not absurd at all, although we can sometimes fail to grasp these meanings. . . . Moreover, as we have seen, we can claim all this with an open and clear scientific conscience. The religious hypothesis, if it does indeed hold that the world is meaningful rather than absurd, is therefore a viable hypothesis for us. There is no scientific reason we cannot believe it.[22]

Polanyi is probably most famous for promoting the idea that all knowledge is personal knowledge, or what he called tacit knowledge. The idea that knowledge is purely information and can be discovered by reason alone, he says, is misguided and naive. It is not how science really works. Science is often defined as the disinterested pursuit of knowledge, but if the scientist is really disinterested, they will not get very far in pursuing new discoveries. Scientists develop convictions and biases about the direction of their research, and the master scientist builds on a lifetime of knowledge and experience, drawing on intuition to select from an infinite number of possible directions they might pursue in solving a problem or developing new theories.

Polanyi argued that "we believe more than we can prove, and we know more than we can tell." All knowledge is tacit, implied, inferred, related to skills, intuition, and experiences, but it is difficult to explain logically to others how we came by it. The extreme rationalization and empirical standards of knowledge in science in the age of Enlightenment have little interest or patience with other forms of knowledge like this.[23]

4. *The Twilight of the Enlightenment*

In our day, we are seeing the fruits of the seventeenth-century Enlightenment with its focus on the autonomous, liberated self. Some voices celebrate the continued triumphs of this movement with great confidence in the "doctrine of progress" that will lead us to even greater heights and to eventually overcome all obstacles.

But the exercise of our own free choices cannot be the ultimate good in life and the final reality. An honest look at our human nature suggests that we are contingent beings, dependent on some greater power that has given us life and continues to sustain us. Dorothy Sayers describes the dilemma of the modern humanist in this way:

> The people who are most discouraged and made despondent by the barbarity and stupidity of human behavior at this time are those who think highly of Homo Sapiens as a product of evolution, and who still cling to an optimistic belief in the civilizing influence of progress and enlightenment. To them, the appalling outbursts of bestial ferocity in the Totalitarian States, and the obstinate selfishness and stupid greed of Capitalist Society, are not merely shocking and alarming. For them, these things are the utter negation of everything in which they have believed. It is as though the bottom had dropped out of their universe. The whole thing looks like a denial of all reason, and they feel as if they and the world had gone mad together.[24]

For an example of this doctrine of progress, see Steven Pinker's writing.[25] Other historians observe that we find ourselves in the twilight of the Enlightenment.[26] The failure of any consensus for the "common good," with individualism gone to seed, leaves us without a moral compass and without a clear foundation for a moral society.[27]

We have seen the rise and fall of utopian dreams, the ravages of totalitarian regimes, and numerous strands of nihilism that invite us simply to give up on our longing for joy. One recent version of this nihilism is what Jonathan Rauch calls "apatheism," a term he coined to describe his own apathetic response to the whole question of God and religion.[28] Who cares about these questions anymore?

We seem to be witnessing a withering of our capacity for joy. But thankfully, the desire for joy and meaning and fullness of life is very resilient. "Human longing cannot be destroyed . . . Nor — and here is the hope — will we ever leave this tortured longing behind."[29] "Fundamentally, the answer to the lies of this world — even the Liar and great imposter himself, Satan — is joy."[30]

5. Re-enchantment: Rediscovering the Transcendent

In the 2007 Disney blockbuster movie *Enchanted*, starring Amy Adams, we see the ingenious mixing of the animated world of fairy tale spilling over into the bustling streets of New York City, where the animated characters become magically transformed into live-action ones. It quickly turns into a riotous fish-out-of-water comedy. The mixing of the real world with the rules of the animated world still at play is somewhat unsettling. The confusion that follows is pure delight, as Disney pokes some fun at itself (*Snow White, Sleeping Beauty*) while experimenting with new technology. This is a love-story musical with a lady in distress, a rescue, and all the other components. The lady, Giselle, is wholesome, the epitome of goodness and innocence — and charming. We have to leave our cynicism behind and let ourselves be caught up in the magic to truly enjoy this film and to be able to catch its message. Giselle is transported into the real world by the wicked queen to prevent her from marrying her stepson, the prince. In the real world there are "no happy endings" and no one is happy for very long. But she is wrong. Giselle instead finds her true love, in the real world. Even the hard-boiled New Yorkers find her joyful enthusiasm contagious, and they are caught up in her vision as she sings her song of true love in Central Park.

This disenchanted world we live in still longs for enchantment, something more than the meaningless life of selfish, self-reliant individuals just looking out for themselves; something more than a materialist view of the universe. As Annie Dillard writes, "You were made and set here to give voice to this, your own astonishment."[31] People long for a transcendent reality that will make sense of their confused, empty, wandering existence. This is not sentimentality. When we sentimentalize, we block out the world with our own preconceived feelings. But when we see the world, when we are fully present, to see it in all of its fullness, in all of its joy, we allow the experience of the world to flood into our whole being.[32]

In 2013 the former archbishop of Canterbury, Rowan Williams, led a large gathering to install a plaque honoring C. S. Lewis in Poets' Corner at Westminster Abbey, commemorating the fiftieth year of Lewis's death. This placed Lewis alongside other notables, such as Chaucer, Dickens, Yeats, Keats, Austen, Shakespeare, and many others. The quote chosen for the plaque is one from Lewis: "I believe in Christianity as I believe the sun has risen. Not only because I can see it but because by it, I can see everything else."

In his famous poem "God's Grandeur," Gerard Manley Hopkins declares, "The world is charged with the grandeur of God." Like electricity or lightning, the world is alive with God's presence. And even though the world is "seared with trade; bleared, smeared with toil,"

> There lives the dearest freshness deep down things;
> And though the last lights off the black West went

Oh, morning, at the brown brink eastward, springs —
Because the Holy Ghost over the bent
World broods with warm breast and with ah!
    bright wings.[33]

Rumors of Another World

We encounter hints and clues scattered all about this world that can point us to the transcendent. Along this line, sociologist Peter Berger outlines five signs in everyday life, "signals of transcendence," that point us to the supernatural — order, play, hope, damnation, and humor. Just to take one example, that of order:

> Throughout most of human history, men have believed that the created order of society, in one way or another, corresponds to an underlying order of the universe, a divine order that supports and justifies all human attempts at ordering. . . . This is the human faith in order as such, a faith closely related to man's fundamental trust in reality. . . . Man's propensity for order is grounded in a faith or trust that, ultimately, reality is "in order," "all right," "as it should be."[34]

We also see clues of the desire for transcendence in popular culture (often unintentionally). We see it in films like *Enchanted*. We see it in *Les Misérables*. We see it again and again in the messianic rescuers of the *Star Wars* series and the superhero messiahs of the Marvel Studios *Avengers* series. Why is it that Hollywood can't seem to help themselves from returning to these well-worn themes? What is it about audiences that they never tire of seeing the conflict between good and evil portrayed on the big screen, with action heroes coming to the rescue?

Why are we so often moved to tears when justice and right prevails in these stories? And why do we still want people to "live happily ever after"? As I have said, the problem with the Hollywood happy endings is not that they are overdone but that they are too timid and faint-hearted, too shy to reach for the real happy ending. Some may attribute our desire for happy endings to sentimentalism, but such endings have a strong appeal deep within the human psyche, and it is not going away. Why?

> Joy to the world, the Lord is come!
> Let earth receive her King;
> Let ev'ry heart prepare him room
> And heaven and nature sing.

Reflection Questions

1. Jesus came to bring joy to the world (Luke 2:10). Why do you think we don't see more of this joy in our world? Does your life reflect this joy?

2. Sometimes it seems like this world is under a spell or asleep, and it needs some kind of powerful wake-up call. How have you seen this in yourself or others?

3. It seems clear that Jesus came not just to reform the world but to redeem the world. How would you describe Jesus's mission on earth? How have you experienced this redemption?

4. In our secular society, the rejection of the supernatural has created a crisis of meaning. How do people you know find a sense of meaning and purpose? What makes life worth living for you?

12

Destined for Joy

We were walking along the ridge of the Continental Divide in the Rocky Mountains. The three of us — my wife and I and a good friend — had begun the ascent before dawn. It would be an all-day hike. And now, here we were at what seemed the top of the world. Looking in one direction, we saw the earth sloping down over hills and valleys. In the other direction a glacier slid down into a lake which, then fed a stream. This view stands as one of the greatest thrills of my life. Well above the timberline, where there is not enough oxygen for trees to grow, the tundra was filled with the loveliest of flowers. It was all so pure, so untouched, so delicate. My heart was bursting with joy. I thought of that first garden. How beautiful it must have been.

> Morning has broken like the first morning;
> Blackbird has spoken like the first bird.

These well-known lyrics were written not by Cat Stevens but by the English hymn writer Eleanor Farjeon in 1931. She was asked to write a song for children, to help them express gratitude every day for God's creation. "Morning has broken like the first morning."

Every morning can remind us of that first morning. Each new day beckons us to remember that first garden, the first bird, the first dewfall on the first grass, where God's feet passed. All subsequent mornings are "born of the one light Eden saw play." Farjeon's beautiful poetry captures the scene so well.

Sometimes when I walk in my neighborhood, especially in springtime, I am struck by the many varieties of flowers and plants, the grass and the trees, the lush greens under the blue sky. Who would have thought there were so many shades of green? My heart is filled with joy. And I sometimes say out loud, "Lord, your garden is still flourishing on this earth." It reminds me of that garden that once was, and it also points me to a new heavens and earth that is yet to come.

If you have ever hiked up a tall mountain or far into a forest that suddenly opens up to a place that is pure and lush, unspoiled by human hands, you may have felt a stirring in your soul, a strange attraction, a yearning to remain there always, almost like you belong there.

Before sin and death entered this world, our first parents lived in paradise in sweet fellowship with their God. The food was there for the picking. The water was pure and refreshing. The garden of God was filled with beauty of every imaginable flower and plant and tree, and rivers and brooks. It was a place of peace — shalom — where all was well, where the worship of God was natural and continuous and joyful. This was God's garden and God's temple. It was a manifestation of the joy we were made for and are destined for.

Are We Home Yet?

All our lives we are searching for a home, a real home, a place of safety, belonging, warmth, welcome, and rest. For some this becomes a literal search, and a restless one, with frequent moves, hoping this next new place will finally be *the one*. It is the hope that just on the far side of that hill, the grass will be greener, life will be better, and we will find our home at last. But it is an illusory hope, and we will always be disappointed. The new house never quite measures up, and soon it is time to move on. I read recently that in any given year, 10 percent of Americans will move into a new house.

For several years, I watched my brother go through this restless phase. Escaping the dull life of the Midwest, he moved his family to Colorado, but his job as a realtor didn't work out, and Denver was crowded. A few years later it was on to Leavenworth, Washington, a lovely Bavarian-style village. But jobs were scarce, and the novelty soon wore off. Then it was on to Southern California. But there the landscapes were too brown; they missed the lush green trees and the changing seasons. So finally it was back to the Midwest, to Michigan. I don't think he ever did find his home.

This joyful longing, or hopeful searching, for a home is repeatedly portrayed in movies, fairy tales, music, art, and novels. For some, the idea of "home" might conjure images of a castle on a hill, or a cottage in the woods, or a house overlooking the sea. For me the picture would be a cabin in the mountains, with a bubbling stream alongside it. As lovely as these pictures are, we won't find the ultimate answer to our longings in them. Still, they serve as pointers to something beyond.

When we are asked, perhaps in a "get acquainted" sort of game, "What do you consider to be your emotional home?," some of us look back on a childhood home with fond memories — maybe the yard, or a special room inside. Or it may be our grandparents' house. Whatever it is, it is a place that played a crucial role in our sense of belonging and security and joy. And that memory sparks a yearning deep within us to find again that kind of emotional home as we continue our journey in life.

But it is our final home that we are really looking for, that place where we weary pilgrims can finally be at rest. If we mistake the shadows for the thing itself, then those shadows become idols and we are likely to settle for something far less than our real home. In popular culture we find signals that can provide clues to the truth and point us in the direction of our deepest longings, but they are not the real deal. Picasso once said, "Art is not truth. Art is a lie that makes us realize truth."[1]

C. S. Lewis called this our longing for a far-off country:

> In speaking of this desire for our own far-off country, which we find in ourselves even now, I feel a certain shyness. I am almost committing an indecency. I am trying to rip open the inconsolable secret in each one of you – the secret which hurts so much that you take your revenge on it by calling it names like Nostalgia and Romanticism and Adolescence; the secret also which pierces with such sweetness that when, in very intimate conversation, the mention of it becomes imminent, we grow awkward and affect a laugh at ourselves; the secret we cannot hide and cannot tell, though we desire to do both. We cannot tell it because it is a desire for something that has never actually appeared in our experience. We cannot hide it because our experience is constantly suggesting it, and we betray ourselves like lovers at the mention of a name.[2]

We see this common theme in the biblical story – that we are wanderers, sojourners, pilgrims, exiles on this earth (Gen. 15:13; Lev. 25:23; Pss. 39:12; 119:19; 1 Pet. 2:11). We are the homeless. This world, at least not in its present form, is not our final home. Sometimes we are forgetful pilgrims, tempted to settle and to latch onto some shadow of a home that will never satisfy our deepest longing.

It is in the epistle to the Hebrews that we find the most direct statement that the heroes of faith were "looking forward to a city that has foundations, whose designer and builder is God" (Heb. 11:10). They were seeking a homeland, a better country.

> These all died in faith, not having received the things promised, but having seen them and greeted them from afar, and having acknowledged that they were *strangers and exiles on the earth.* For people who speak thus make it clear that they are seeking a *homeland.* If they had been thinking of that land from which they had gone out, they would have had opportunity to return. But as it is, they desire a *better country,* that is, *a heavenly one.* Therefore God is not ashamed to be called their God, for he has *prepared for them a city.* (Heb. 11:13–16; cf. 12:22–24; 13:13–14; emphasis mine)

In the final book of the Narnia tales, *The Last Battle,* as the Narnians are rushing into the new Narnia, Lewis has the unicorn say these amazing words:

> I have come home at last! This is my real country! I belong here. This is the land I have been looking for all my life, though I never knew it till now. The reason why we loved the old Narnia is that it sometimes looked a little like this. Bree-hee-hee! Come further up, come further in![3]

In relation to this idea of a final home, Lewis and others often used the German word *Sehnsucht,* which refers to an inconsolable longing, an ache, a yearning, and wonder. It is difficult to describe and is best conveyed by poets. It is a bit like nostalgia, though not for some past experience but for a future reality not yet realized. It suggests a sense of separation from what is deeply desired. A ceaseless longing that points beyond us. When we reflect on this longing, our hearts are bursting with joy. The great composers Schubert, Wagner, Beethoven, and Strauss incorporated the theme of *Sehnsucht* into their music. "Human longing cannot be destroyed; we will always want an infinite end." And this is why the voices of nihilism will not prevail. Richard J. Neuhaus says it so well:[4]

> For paradise we long. For perfection we were made. We don't know what it would be like or feel like, but we must settle for nothing less. This longing is the source of the hunger and dissatisfaction that mark our lives; it drives our ambition. What we long for is touched in our exaltations; in our devastations it is known by its absence. This longing makes our loves and friendships possible, and so very unsatisfactory. The hunger is for nothing less than paradise, nothing less than perfect communion with the Absolute — with the Good, the True, the Beautiful — communion with the perfectly One in whom all the fragments of our scattered existence come together at last and forever. We must not stifle this longing. It is a holy dissatisfaction. Such dissatisfaction is not a sickness to be healed, but the seed of a promise to be fulfilled.
> ... The only death to fear is the death of settling for something less.[5]

Dr. Martyn Lloyd-Jones comments that there is a similar word in Welsh, *hiraeth*, that can be translated "homesickness." It is the consciousness of being apart from one's home, very similar to a Christian's yearning for heaven.

Christian Hope Is Not Escapist

There is a common notion about Christians who believe in a world to come, that they are "so heavenly minded they are no earthly

good." And there may be some for whom this is true. But I want
to propose that it is only those who are heavenly minded who can
be any earthly good. To be heavenly minded, to fix your mind on
things above, on the spiritual realities of what God has accomplished in Jesus Christ, to be mindful that God is preparing a new
heavens and new earth, a place of love and peace and justice and
righteousness — that can be a powerful driving force for our in-
volvement in this world. It is also a great incentive for holy living
and healthy relationships (Col. 3). I have come to think of Christian discipleship not so much as something we are pushed into,
but rather something we are pulled into; as being pulled into our
future destiny.

In the 1960s Pete Seeger and others spoke of religion as "pie in
the sky in the sweet by and by — that's a lie." It was a variation of a
song by Joe Hill, which was a parody of the Christian hymn "In the
Sweet By and By." Concerned over the terrible plight of migrant
workers, Hill sang, "You will eat, by and by / In that glorious land
above the sky / Work and pray, live on hay / You'll get pie in the
sky when you die." The peril of migrant workers continues to be an
injustice to this day, one that Christians must address.

When I first heard these words, I was not a believer, and I remember being so impressed by the boldness of the slogan and
thought it was cool. Of course, this was picking up on Marx's
claim that religion is the opium of the people. The view was that
the dream of heaven is just a way for the evil aristocracy to keep
the masses compliant and passive rather than working for a better
world now. Religion is escapist and does not engage in the injus-
tices against and suffering of common people. Religion is just sappy
sentimentalism. And of course, there was and still is some truth to
this, as it is practiced by some religious groups. No doubt many
enslavers in the antebellum period presented reminders of heaven

just to keep the people they were enslaving in line. But this is not the biblical view of heaven.

The Bible never speaks of the Christian hope as an escape from this world and certainly not as an excuse to exploit people in this life. Quite the opposite, the vision of the new heavens and the new earth is actually very earthy and filled with references to justice and making things right, as well as judgment for evil oppressors. The messianic kingdom is characterized by justice and righteousness, from the very first prophecies about a coming Messiah, to the cry of the prophets for earthly justice now, to the final vision of the eternal kingdom.

> "For to us a child is born,
>   to us a son is given;
> and the government shall be upon his shoulder,
>   and his name shall be called
> Wonderful Counselor, Mighty God,
>   Everlasting Father, Prince of Peace.
> Of the increase of his government and of peace
>   there will be no end,
> on the throne of David and over his kingdom,
>   to establish it and to uphold it
> with justice and with righteousness
>   from this time forth and forevermore.
> The zeal of the LORD of hosts will do this." (Isa. 9:6–7)

> "He shall not judge by what his eyes see,
>   or decide disputes by what his ears hear,
> but with righteousness he shall judge the poor,
>   and decide with equity for the meek of the earth;
> and he shall strike the earth with the rod of his mouth,

and with the breath of his lips he shall kill
the wicked.
Righteousness shall be the belt of his waist,
and faithfulness the belt of his loins." (Isa. 11:3–5)

Thus says the LORD:
"Keep justice, and do righteousness,
for soon my salvation will come,
and my righteousness be revealed." (Isa. 56:1)

"The Spirit of the Lord GOD is upon me,
because the Lord has anointed me
to bring good news to the poor;
he has sent me to bind up the brokenhearted,
to proclaim liberty to the captives,
and the opening of the prison to those who are
bound." (Isa. 61:1)

"For I the LORD love justice;
I hate robbery and wrong;
I will faithfully give them their recompense,
and I will make an everlasting covenant
with them."   (Isa. 61:8)

"The wolf and the lamb shall graze together;
the lion shall eat straw like the ox,
and dust shall be the serpent's food.
They shall not hurt or destroy
in all my holy mountain." (Isa. 76:25)

This vision of God's ultimate plan for a kingdom of love and
peace and joy, a new heavens and earth, a new city, can and must

spill over into our present mission on this earth. If God is finally going to bring about perfect justice and righteousness and peace, then surely this must characterize our mission now. As the widely circulated quote (attributed to Augustine) goes, "Hope has two lovely daughters — their names are anger and courage; anger at the way things are, courage to change it."[6] This ultimate hope can give us a healthy dissatisfaction with the current state of our world. In working toward change, however, we must avoid the mistakes of the past. We must not turn this into a new "social gospel," assuming that we can do this in our own power and might. This must be a supernatural work of God, and it is God's grace working through us that will bring about real change. We cannot assume that people's lives can flourish apart from a personal, living, saving relationship with the God who made them.

The message of prophets like Micah and Amos centers on justice in the here and now. "Let justice roll down like waters, and righteousness like an ever-flowing stream" (Amos 5:24). "He has told you, O man, what is good; and what does the LORD require of you but to do justice, and to love kindness, and to walk humbly with your God?" (Mic. 6:8). "Learn to do right; seek justice. Defend the oppressed. Take up the cause of the fatherless; plead the case of the widow" (Isa. 1:17). As missionaries have gone to other countries, their gospel ministry has almost always been accompanied by establishing schools, hospitals, and clinics; teaching farming techniques; encouraging local businesses; digging wells; and sometimes challenging corrupt national leaders.

Once again, Joni Eareckson Tada is a great example of someone who does earthly good precisely *because* she is heavenly minded. She is always talking and singing about heaven, but she has been a world leader in defending the rights of disabled people, providing education, advocacy, Wheels for the World, legal support, and much more. She is now facing her second cancer diagnosis, on top of the long-term effects on her heart for having been a quadriplegic for fifty years. Her response? "Life is worth nothing unless I use it for doing the work assigned me by the Lord Jesus — the work of telling others the Good News about God's almighty kindness and love" (Acts 20:24 TLB).

At this point in our discussion, the themes of joy and hope are very closely intertwined. Can we live without hope? Not for long. In a real sense, I do what I hope, and I hope what I do. Hope is as necessary to life as light and air. It is essential to the experience of joy. Biblical hope is not the hope that is so common in our world; it is bold and robust. It produces courage and perseverance. Hope keeps us from growing weary in well-doing (Gal. 6:9). "Hope is nothing else than the expectation of things that faith has believed to be truly promised by God."[7]

Your Eschatology Is Showing

Eschatology is the branch of theology that has to do with the final events in history and the ultimate destiny of humanity. Everyone has an eschatology. What one believes about the afterlife has serious ramifications for how one lives this life. Everyone's outlook on life is shaped by their eschatology, though not everyone realizes it. Not everyone lives consistently with that picture.

I was living in England in 1999 when Glenn Hoddle was the very popular coach of England's football (soccer) team as they headed into the European Cup. It was generally known that he believed in karma and reincarnation, but he made the mistake of saying publicly that he believed disabled people were being punished in this life for sins committed in a previous life. There was such an uproar over this that he was removed from his coaching position. It was a grim reminder that one's view of the afterlife has ramifications for this life.

When Princess Diana was tragically killed in a car crash in 1997, it shook the whole country — the whole world, to some extent. The royal family grossly underestimated how much Diana had captured the hearts of the British people. People lined up for hours outside the palace, placing thousands of flower arrangements, notes, and poems at the palace gates. It was not surprising that the "people's princess" should have evoked such heartfelt sentiment. But the kind of comments left in the notes reflected the shallow understanding of the afterlife that even many who call themselves Christians embrace. One note is representative of many others, written in Diana's voice:

"I did not leave you at all. I am still with you. I am in the sun and in the wind. I am even in the rain. I did not die. I am with you all."

I continue to be amazed by how many Christians view heaven as a place where we will all live some ghostlike, ethereal, floating-on-clouds existence rather than holding to the distinctly Christian doctrine of the resurrection of the body. The relationship between this world and the next is one of continuity and discontinuity. That is, the new heavens and the new earth is not simply a remodeled version of this earth, but one that is purged, radically transformed, even burned, but then renewed. As with our earthly bodies and glorified bodies, we have continuity *and* transformation (Rom. 8:18–24; 1 Cor. 15:35–48).

We have seen that promises of Marxist utopian dreams, heaven-on-earth dreams, have failed to deliver. Marxist regimes just traded one oppressive system for another. As in George Orwell's *Animal Farm*, the new socialist rulers soon began to look and behave very much like the previous capitalist ones they had overthrown. The twentieth century is littered with failed Marxist experiments under Stalin and Mao and the Khmer Rouge, with their gulags and famines and killing fields that left more than one hundred million people dead.

We might ask, What is the eschatology of scientific materialism? What is the fate of the universe and how will it all end according to the scenarios spun out by the cosmologists? Without the intervention of God, there is no purely scientific basis for a hope in the perpetuation of the universe.

All forecasts of the future, whether they are made for living beings, planets, stars, galaxies, or universes, point toward disintegration: the sun will cool down, earth will be lost in space, and even the matter of the universe will undergo radioactive decay. For this reason, there is no scientific basis for hope.[8]

As John Polkinghorne and Michael Welker comment, "A universe moving from big bang to hot death or cosmic crunch hardly seems to lend comfort to the human heart."[9] In spite of this grim reality, some with this worldview are driven to desperate heroism or stoic defiance. Others may find a cause in life that is big enough to consume their energies and ambitions.

Others look to artificial intelligence as the hope of the future, to usher in a utopian era, perhaps one with robots replacing human beings. More recently, we are seeing the Silicon Valley vision: eternal youth, perpetual health and vitality in this life. Leaders in technology, such as Google's cofounders, who find it unacceptable that 150,000 people die every day and who don't intend to be included in that sorry group, are on a quest to end aging forever and finally attain eternal life.[10]

We must not be shy in talking about heaven simply because it is not fashionable today, even in some Christian circles. But for those who have suffered much, for those who have refused to "settle" in this world, who have not been enamored with the cheap offerings on display in our affluent culture, the promise of a new heavens and new earth is wonderful and joyous.

We taste joy in this life that is sweet and real but always fleeting and intermittent. But the clear, consistent promise of the eternal kingdom is "everlasting joy."

> And the ransomed of the LORD shall return
> and come to Zion with singing;
> *everlasting joy* shall be upon their heads;
> they shall obtain *gladness and joy*,
> and sorrow and sighing shall flee away.
>
> (Isa. 35:10; cf. 51:11; emphasis mine)

> Instead of your shame there shall be a double portion;
> instead of dishonor they shall *rejoice* in their lot;
> therefore in their land they shall possess a
> double portion;
> they shall have *everlasting joy*.
>
> (Isa. 61:7, emphasis mine)

What if we presented this kind of picture of the Christian hope to the unbelieving world? Instead of some anemic, ghostlike view of heaven, what if we presented the robust, full, rich-in-beauty, beaming, bustling city of God? What if we presented something that actually corresponded to people's deepest longings?

What Is the Real Happy Ending?

I will tell you honestly: I am longing for the happy ending of the fairy tales — not the Hollywood version of "happily ever after," but *really* living happily ever after, where the good finally triumphs, where justice is finally realized, where friends are reunited, where people can live together in peace and harmony and do meaningful creative work, in perfect communion with the God who made us.

When I was a young man and would see old men welling up with tears at some movie or story where the underdog wins, the lost is found, the wayward one is restored, the unrecognized receive their reward, I would think that he was just a sentimental old fool. But now I suspect that men like that were closer to understanding a deeper reality than a young punk like me could have appreciated at the time. Now I find myself tearing up more easily at these same things.

Why do these kinds of stories capture our imagination at such a deep level?

- Once upon a time, a little girl named Lucy was playing hide-and-seek with her brothers and sister and decided to hide in a wardrobe, and she discovered a whole new world.
- Once upon a time there was an old king named King Lear, and he had three daughters. Two of them flattered him but did not love him, and one was stubborn and spoke her mind, but she loved him most sincerely, and as he lay dying, he finally saw the truth.

Throughout history, God has sent humanity pictures, archetypes, signals, pointers that arouse in us longings that cannot be fulfilled in this world. The kingdom of heaven is buried like a treasure in this world, and it is there to be found.[11]

J. R. R. Tolkien coined the term "eucatastrophe" (good catastrophe) to explain the sudden turn of events in a fairy tale where what appears to be a catastrophe turns out to be the very opposite.

It is the mark of a good fairy-story, of the higher or more complete kind, that however wild its events, however fantastic or terrible its adventures, it can give to a child or man that hears it,

when the "turn" comes, a catch of the breath, a beat and lifting
of the heart, near to (or indeed accompanied by) tears, as keen
as that given by any form of literary art.[12]

He elaborates further on this idea in relation to the Christian story
in a letter to his son Christopher:

> The Resurrection was the greatest 'eucatastrophe' possible in the
> greatest Fairy Story — and produces that essential emotion: Chris-
> tian joy which produces tears because it is qualitatively so like
> sorrow, because it comes from those places where Joy and Sorrow
> are at one, reconciled, as selfishness and altruism are lost in Love.[13]

In the fairy tale, the beast becomes beautiful, the cowardly lion
becomes brave, the selfish boy is transformed, and the exiled king
is finally restored in the land of Gondor.

Frederick Buechner calls preachers to greater boldness in telling
this greatest story of all that is "too good not to be true."

> Let him preach this overwhelming of tragedy by comedy, of
> darkness by light, of the ordinary by the extraordinary, as the
> tale that is too good not to be true because to dismiss it as untrue
> is to dismiss along with it that "catch of the breath, that beat and
> lifting of the heart near to or even accompanied by tears," which
> I believe is the deepest intuition of truth that we have.[14]

Here Comes the Bridegroom

Some of my fondest childhood memories are when my family attended weddings. My father was a musician, and sometimes he
played in a band at these weddings. There is something about a
wedding feast (any feast really, but especially a wedding feast),

something magical. It lifts our spirits, it brings joy to our hearts, it is a festive, happy occasion. It is also often a majestic affair. The bride enters in a flowing white gown. The groom never looked so good in his tuxedo and shiny shoes. The grand wedding march is thrilling. The bridesmaids wear colorful dresses, and the grooms-men, tuxes. The reception is filled with laughter, speeches, music, and dancing. The food is good, the wine is flowing, the bride and groom are euphoric, the guests are jubilant. I would often look around to see faces filled with joy.

And so I am understandably delighted to know that at the end of time, the consummation of God's eternal kingdom will begin with a wedding feast — the greatest wedding feast ever — the marriage feast of the Lamb (Rev. 19). The prophet Isaiah spoke of this great feast, at which God will "swallow up death forever and the LORD God will wipe away tears from all faces" (Isa. 25:6–9). Besides his famous miracle at the wedding at Cana (John 2), Jesus often told stories of wedding feasts (Matt. 8:11; 22:2; 25:10; Luke 12:35), and at the Last Supper Jesus told his disciples, "I will not again drink of the fruit of the vine until I drink it new with you in my Father's kingdom" (Matt. 26:29).

Throughout Scripture, Christ is presented as the bridegroom, and the church is the bride (Eph. 5:25–33; Matt. 9:15; John 3:29). Scripture is pointing ahead to that great wedding feast of the Lamb when this marriage will finally be consummated. Finally, in Revelation 19, the bride is ready, multitudes have gathered, and the king, who is the groom, rides in on a white horse.

> Then I heard what seemed to be the voice of a great multitude,
> like the roar of many waters and like the sound of mighty peals
> of thunder, crying out,

"Hallelujah!
For the Lord our God
　　the Almighty reigns.
Let us rejoice and exult
　　and give him the glory,
for the marriage of the Lamb has come,
　　and his Bride has made herself ready;
it was granted her to clothe herself
　　with fine linen, bright and pure" —

for the fine linen is the righteous deeds of the saints.

　　And the angel said to me, "Write this: Blessed are those who are invited to the marriage supper of the Lamb." And he said to me, "These are the true words of God." (Rev. 19:6–9)

Never has there been a grander wedding feast than the marriage supper of the Lamb. Never has there been a more diverse guest list, and never have people been more blessed to receive an invitation to attend. The invitation in their hands (as I picture it) is dipped in blood and bears the symbol of the cross and the crown. There will be people gathered from every tribe and language and people and nation (Rev. 5:9; 13:7). This guest list will include patriarchs and elders, saints and martyrs, nobles and peasants, and wayward sons and daughters who have come home at last. They all have one thing in common: they worship the Lamb, and they owe him everything. And together they form the lovely bride of Christ.

　　And Jesus, the Lamb of God who takes away the sin of the world, now is revealed as King of kings and Lord of lords. He sits on a white horse as the warrior king, the bridegroom attended by armies of angels. And they will put a final end to war and rebellion.

I am reminded of the seventies song "God and Man at Table Are Sat Down." It is often sung in connection with the Lord's Supper, but its ultimate reference is to the marriage feast of the Lamb.

> O welcome, all ye noble saints of old,
> As now before your very eyes unfold
> . . . .
> God and man at table are sat down.[15]

The song goes on to speak of how this earth shall pass away, Jesus and the Bride will arrive for the great wedding feast, to usher a new day and a new beginning.

And in the end, suffering is gathered into joy, despair into hope, sighing into laughter, heaviness into levity, waiting into fulfillment, and death into life.

Death is not the last word. Life is the last word.

Actually, Jesus has the last word for us: "Well done, good and faithful servant. . . . Enter into the joy of your Lord" (Matt. 25:21).

Not *The End*

Reflection Questions

1. As you look back on your life, is there a place that you think of as your emotional home, that place where you once felt safe and secure, that you belonged there?

2. Do you think that this longing for a final, permanent home is something that God uses to point you to your ultimate heavenly home? How would you describe this longing in your own heart?

3. If heaven is a place of love and peace and justice, how does this

motivate you to be active in pursuing these qualities in the world today?

4. How do the promises of everlasting joy in a new heavens and new earth rise above the Hollywood happy endings? How would you describe your own hope beyond this life?

5. Can you imagine how you would feel to see your name printed on an invitation to that great wedding feast of the Lamb at the end of time? How would you describe the feeling?

Notes

Introduction

1. Frederick Buechner, *The Longing for Home: Recollections and Reflections* (San Francisco: HarperSanFrancisco, 1996), 128.

2. Miroslav Volf, "The Crown of the Good Life: A Hypothesis," in *Joy and Human Flourishing: Essays on Theology, Culture, and the Good Life*, ed. Miroslav Volf and Justin E. Crisp (Minneapolis: Fortress Press, 2015), 135.

3. C. S. Lewis, *Surprised by Joy: The Shape of My Early Life* (New York: HarperCollins, 1955), 220–21. Hereafter, page references to this work will be placed in the text.

4. Lewis outlines these other philosophies in his early book *The Pilgrim's Regress*.

5. C. S. Lewis, *Mere Christianity* (New York: HarperOne, 1952), 120.

6. George MacDonald, *Adela Cathcart* (Whitehorn, CA: Johannesen, 1994), 6.

7. Alexander Schmemann, *For the Life of the World: Sacraments and Orthodoxy* (1963; repr., Yonkers, NY: St. Vladimir's Seminary Press, 2018).

8. Charles Mathewes, "Toward a Theology of Joy," in Volf and Crisp, *Joy and Human Flourishing*.

9. Mathewes, "Toward a Theology of Joy," 83.

Chapter 1

1. Frederick Buechner, *The Longing for Home: Recollections and Reflections* (San Francisco: HarperSanFrancisco, 1996), 112.

2. H. Van Broekhoven Jr., "Joy," in *The International Standard Bible Encyclopedia* (Grand Rapids: Eerdmans, 1982), 2:1140.

3. In the construction of Hebrew parallelism, the words "dancing" and "joy" are presented as synonyms.

4. J. Alec Motyer, *The Prophecy of Isaiah: An Introduction and Commentary* (Downers Grove, IL: InterVarsity Press, 1993), 452–53.

5. Motyer, *Prophecy of Isaiah*, 458.

6. Dick Lucas and Christopher Green, *The Message of 2 Peter and Jude* (The Bible Speaks Today) (Downers Grove, IL: IVP Academic, 1995), 233.

7. James Denney, *Studies in Theology* (London: Hodder and Stoughton, 1904), 171.

8. Jürgen Moltmann, "Christianity: A Religion of Joy," in *Joy and Human Flourishing: Essays on Theology, Culture, and the Good Life*, ed. Miroslav Volf and Justin E. Crisp (Minneapolis: Fortress Press, 2015).

9. Joseph Cardinal Ratzinger, *Principles of Catholic Theology: Building Stones for a Fundamental Theology* (San Francisco: Ignatius Press, 1987), 78.

10. "Held Hostage," Act Three, *This American Life*, episode 409, June 4, 2010, www.thisamericanlife.org/409/held-hostage/act-three-7.

11. *Ode to Joy*, directed by Jason Winer (IFC Films, 2019).

Chapter 2

1. *BBC*, January 11, 2007, www.bbc.co.uk/films/2007/01/08/the _pursuit_of_happyness_2007_review.shtml.

2. Mary Clark Moschella, "Elements of Joy in Lived Practices of Care," in *Joy and Human Flourishing: Essays on Theology, Culture, and the*

Good Life, ed. Miroslav Volf and Justin E. Crisp (Minneapolis: Fortress Press, 2015), 100.

3. C. S. Lewis, *The Screwtape Letters* (New York: Harper, 1942), Letter 9.

4. John Calvin, *Commentary on the Psalms*, abridged by David C. Searle (Edinburgh: Banner of Truth, 2009), 49.

5. David Brooks, *The Second Mountain: The Quest for a Moral Life* (New York: Random House, 2019), xxxiii.

6. Brené Brown, *Daring Greatly: How the Courage to Be Vulnerable Transforms the Way We Live, Love, Parent, and Lead* (New York: Penguin Random House, 2012), 123.

7. C. S. Lewis, *Surprised by Joy: The Shape of My Early Life* (New York: HarperCollins, 1955), 72.

8. C. S. Lewis, *Christian Behaviour*, in *The Best of C. S. Lewis* (New York: Iversen Associates, 1969), 504.

9. Lewis, *Christian Behaviour*, 505.

10. Mike Mason, *Champagne for the Soul: Rediscovering God's Gift of Joy* (Vancouver: Regent College Publishing, 2006), 1.

11. Kay Warren, *Joy Is a Choice You Can Make Today* (Grand Rapids, MI: Revell, 2016).

12. C. S. Lewis, *The Weight of Glory, and Other Addresses* (New York: HarperCollins, 1949), 26.

13. Miroslav Volf, "The Crown of the Good Life: A Hypothesis," in *Joy and Human Flourishing*, 135.

14. Her popular twenty-minute TED Talk "The Power of Vulnerability," from January 3, 2011, is definitely worth the time to listen: www.youtube.com/watch?v=iCvmsMzlF7o.

Chapter 3

1. Steve Wilkens, *What's So Funny about God? A Theological Look at Humor* (Downers Grove, IL: InterVarsity Press, 2019).

2. Donald Sweeting, "The Humor of Christ," National Association of Evangelicals, www.nae.org/the-humor-of-christ.

3. Wilkens, *What's So Funny about God?*, 86–88.

Chapter 4

1. Earl Palmer, *Laughter in Heaven: Understanding the Parables of Jesus* (Vancouver: Regent College Publishing, 2004), 32.

2. "I Sought the Lord, and Afterward I Knew," written around 1878, is based on 1 John 4:19.

3. He made this comment at a conference, but see his book *He Has Made Me Glad: Enjoying God's Goodness with Reckless Delight* (Downers Grove, IL: InterVarsity Press, 2005).

4. J. R. R. Tolkien, *The Fellowship of the Ring, Being the First Part of The Lord of the Rings* (Boston: Houghton Mifflin, 1965), 241–47.

Chapter 5

1. Quoted by Glenn Edward Sadler in his introduction to George MacDonald, *The Gifts of the Child Christ: Fairy Tales and Stories for the Childlike* (Grand Rapids, MI: Eerdmans, 1972).

2. Daniel Gabelman, *George MacDonald: Divine Carelessness and Fairy Tale Levity* (Waco, TX: Baylor University Press, 2013), 99.

3. G. K. Chesterton, "George MacDonald and His Work," *The (London) Daily News,* June 11, 1901.

4. "Simple Twist of Fate," released in 1975 on *Blood on the Tracks.*

5. *Children's Letters to God*, compiled by Eric Marshall and Stuart Hample (New York: Simon and Schuster, 1967).

6. Robert Fulghum, *All I Really Needed to Know I Learned in Kindergarten* (New York: Ballantine Books, 1989).

7. Mayra Mendez, PhD, LMFT, quoted in Kimberly Zapata, "The Importance of Play: How Kids Learn by Having Fun," *Healthline*, Sep-

tember 28, 2020, www.healthline.com/health/the-importance-of-play
#benefits.

8. Sam Wang and Sandra Aamodt, "Play, Stress, and the Learning Brain," *Cerebrum*, September–October 2012, www.ncbi.nlm.nih.gov /pmc/articles/PMC3574776.

9. Gabelman, *George MacDonald*, 103.

Chapter 6

1. Abraham Joshua Heschel, *Sabbath* (New York: Farrar, Straus and Giroux, 1951).

2. Timothy Keller, *The King's Cross: Understanding the Life and Death of the Son of God* (New York: Penguin Random House, 2011), 43.

3. George Herbert, "Gratefulness," in *The English Poems of George Herbert* (London: J. M. Dent and Sons, 1974), 134–35. The quote here is just an excerpt from the poem. The rest is well worth reading.

4. Mike Mason, *Champagne for the Soul: Rediscovering God's Gift of Joy* (Vancouver: Regent College Publishing, 2006), 49.

Chapter 7

1. J. R. R. Tolkien, *The Fellowship of the Ring, Being the First Part of The Lord of the Rings* (Boston: Houghton Mifflin, 1965), 60.

2. M. Scott Peck, *The Road Less Traveled: A New Psychology of Love, Traditional Values, and Spiritual Growth* (New York: Simon and Schuster, 1978).

3. See the excellent book by Kathleen Norris, *Acedia and Me: A Marriage, Monks, and a Writer's Life* (New York: Riverhead Books, 2008), where she refers to *acedia* as a "silent despair." Also Rebecca Konyndyk DeYoung, *Glittering Vices: A New Look at the Seven Deadly Sins and Their Remedies* (Grand Rapids, MI: Brazos Press, 2009).

4. Address given to the Public Morality Council, October 23, 1941, reproduced in Dorothy L. Sayers, *Creed or Chaos? Why Christians Must*

Choose Either Dogma or Disaster; Or, Why It Really Does Matter What You Believe (Manchester, NH: Sophia Institute Press, 1995).

5. Mike Mason, *Champagne for the Soul: Rediscovering God's Gift of Joy* (Vancouver: Regent College Publishing, 2006), 45.

6. Mason, *Champagne for the Soul*, 36.

7. Corrie Ten Boom, *He Cares, He Comforts* (Old Tappan, NJ: Fleming H. Revell, 1977), 83.

8. Brené Brown, *Daring Greatly: How the Courage to Be Vulnerable Transforms the Way We Live, Love, Parent, and Lead* (New York: Penguin Random House, 2012), 123.

9. Brown, *Daring Greatly*, 122.

10. Peter Leithart, *Solomon Among the Postmoderns* (Grand Rapids, MI: Brazos Press, 2008), 167.

11. Martin Luther, *The Sermon on the Mount and The Magnificat*, ed. Jaroslav Pelikan, vol. 21 of *Luther's Works* (St. Louis: Concordia, 1956), 197–98.

12. C. H. Spurgeon, *The Gospel of the Kingdom: A Popular Exposition of the Gospel according to Matthew* (New York: Baker & Taylor, 1893), 75.

13. Spoken at a conference but also found in Rebecca Manley Pippert, *Out of the Saltshaker and Into the World: Evangelism as a Way of Life* (Downers Grove, IL: InterVarsity Press, 1979).

14. Timothy Keller, *The Prodigal God: Recovering the Heart of the Christian* Faith (New York: Dutton, 2008).

Chapter 8

1. Alexander Schmemann, *The Journals of Father Alexander Schmemann, 1973–1983* (New York: St. Vladimir's Seminary Press, 2000), 137.

2. Marianne Meye Thompson, "Reflections on Joy in the Bible," in *Joy and Human Flourishing: Essays on Theology, Culture, and the Good Life*, ed. Miroslav Volf and Justin E. Crisp (Minneapolis: Fortress Press, 2015), 20.

3. Ann Voskamp, *One Thousand Gifts: A Dare to Live Fully Right Where You Are* (Nashville: Thomas Nelson, 2011), 84.

4. Timothy Keller, *Walking with God through Pain and Suffering* (New York: Riverhead Books, 2015), 1–3.

5. M. Scott Peck, *People of the Lie: The Hope of Healing Human Evil* (New York: Touchstone Books, 1998). Peck shares his spiritual journey and conversion to Christianity in the introduction.

6. Greek *hēgeomai*.

7. "Joni's Story," http://joniearecksontadastory.com/joni-tadas -story-page-2.

8. "Joni's Story."

9. "A Lifeline When We're Drowning in Hurts: Joni Eareckson Tada and Dedee & Greg Lhamon," *Jesus Calling* (podcast), episode 120, www .jesuscalling.com/blog/lifeline-drowning-hurts-joni-eareckson-tada -dedee-greg-lhamon.

10. C. S. Lewis, *The Problem of Pain* (New York: HarperCollins, 1940), 91.

11. "Joni's Story."

12. Keller, *Walking with God*, chapter 3.

13. C. S. Lewis, *The Weight of Glory, and Other Addresses* (New York: HarperCollins, 1949).

14. Lewis, *The Weight of Glory*, 39–41.

15. "A Lifeline When We're Drowning."

Chapter 9

1. Quoted in Nigel Tomes, "Courage for Christ: The Life of C. T. Studd," www.biblerays.com/uploads/8/0/4/2/8042023/courage_for _christ_ctstudd.pdf.

2. David Brooks, *The Second Mountain: The Quest for a Moral Life* (New York: Random House, 2019), 311.

3. Harvey Cox, *Turning East: The Promise and Peril of the New Orientalism* (New York: Simon and Schuster, 1977).

4. Francine Du Plessix Gray, "God-Watching in America," The Literary View, *New York Times*, December 25, 1977, 136, www.nytimes.com/1977/12/25/archives/the-literary-view-godwatching-in-america-literary-view.html.

5. Malcolm Muggeridge, *Something Beautiful for God: Mother Teresa of Calcutta* (San Francisco: Harper and Row, 1971).

6. Muggeridge, *Something Beautiful for God*, 125.

7. Muggeridge, *Something Beautiful for God*, 114.

8. Malcolm Muggeridge, *Jesus Rediscovered* (Carol Steam, IL: Tyndale, 1973).

9. Mary Clark Moschella, "Elements of Joy in Lived Practices of Care," in *Joy and Human Flourishing: Essays on Theology, Culture, and the Good Life*, ed. Miroslav Volf and Justin E. Crisp (Minneapolis: Fortress Press, 2015), 98.

10. Richard John Neuhaus, "We Shall Not Weary, We Shall Not Rest" (closing address), National Right to Life Convention, Arlington, VA, July 2008.

11. Tracy Kidder, *Mountains Beyond Mountains: The Quest of Dr. Paul Farmer, a Man Who Would Cure the World* (New York: Random House, 2004).

12. Moschella, "Elements of Joy."

13. Mihaly Csikszentmihalyi, *Flow: The Psychology of Optimal Experience* (New York: Harper and Row, 1990).

14. Frederick Buechner, *Wishful Thinking: A Seeker's ABC* (New York: Harper, 1993), 118.

Chapter 10

1. Alexander Schmemann, *For the Life of the World: Sacraments and*

Orthodoxy (1963; repr., Yonkers, NY: St. Vladimir's Seminary Press, 2018), introduction.

2. Charles Mathewes, "Toward a Theology of Joy," in *Joy and Human Flourishing: Essays on Theology, Culture, and the Good Life*, ed. Miroslav Volf and Justin E. Crisp (Minneapolis: Fortress Press, 2015), 65.

3. Rich Nathan, *Empowered Evangelicals: Bringing Together the Best of the Evangelical and Charismatic World* (Boise, ID: Ampelon Publishing, 1995).

4. Jürgen Moltmann, "Christianity: A Religion of Joy," in Volf and Crisp, *Joy and Human Flourishing*, 3.

5. Heidi Neumark, *Breathing Space: A Spiritual Journey in the South Bronx* (Boston: Beacon Press, 2004), 31.

6. David Bentley Hart, *The Experience of God: Being, Consciousness, and Bliss* (New Haven, CT: Yale University Press, 2013).

7. Gregory Beale, *We Become What We Worship: A Biblical Theology of Idolatry* (Downers Grove, IL: InterVarsity Press, 2008), 49.

8. Moltmann, "Christianity," 2–3.

9. Mathewes, "Toward a Theology of Joy," 67.

10. Paul Williams, *Dylan — What Happened?* (New York: Entwhistle Books, 1980), 98.

Chapter 11

1. Pope Francis, *The Joy of the Gospel: Evangelii Gaudium* (Washington, DC: United States Council of Catholic Bishops, 2013). Hereafter, page references to this work will be placed in the text.

2. Greg Forster makes a compelling argument for this in his book *Joy for the World: How Christianity Lost Its Cultural Influence and Can Begin Rebuilding It* (Wheaton, IL: Crossway, 2014).

3. Forster, *Joy for the World*, 279.

4. David Kinnaman, *unChristian: What a New Generation Really*

Thinks About Christianity and Why It Matters (Grand Rapids, MI: Baker Books, 2007).

5. *Trinity Hymnal* (Atlanta: Great Commission Publications, 1990), 195.

6. Alexander Schmemann, *For the Life of the World: Sacraments and Orthodoxy* (1963; repr., Yonkers, NY: St. Vladimir's Seminary Press, 2018).

7. See also the picture of the flourishing life promised in Ezekiel 34:12–15, 25–31.

8. C. S. Lewis, *The Weight of Glory, and Other Addresses* (New York: HarperCollins, 1949), 31.

9. Keith Green, "Your Love Broke Through" (1970), with Randy Stonehill.

10. Frederick Buechner, *The Longing for Home: Recollections and Reflections* (San Francisco: HarperSanFrancisco, 1996), 162.

11. C. S. Lewis, *Mere Christianity*, book 2, chapter 2.

12. Thomas Merton, *The Seven Storey Mountain* (New York: Harcourt Brace, 1948; repr., New York: Harcourt, 1999), 190.

13. Charles Taylor, *A Secular Age* (Cambridge, MA: The Belknap Press of Harvard University Press, 2007).

14. Taylor, *A Secular Age*, 3.

15. Max Weber developed the idea of the Protestant work ethic in *The Protestant Ethic and the "Spirit" of Capitalism: And Other Writings*, trans. Peter Baehr and Gordon Wells (New York: Penguin Books, 2002).

16. Peter Berger, *A Rumor of Angels: Modern Society and the Rediscovery of the Supernatural* (New York: Anchor Books / Doubleday, 1969), 6, 40–41.

17. Max Weber, "Science as a Vocation" (lecture), University of Munich, 1917.

18. C. S. Lewis, *The Abolition of Man* (New York: Harper, 1944), 34–35.

19. Charles Mathewes, "Toward a Theology of Joy," in *Joy and Hu-*

man Flourishing: Essays on Theology, Culture, and the Good Life, ed. Miro-slav Volf and Justin E. Crisp (Minneapolis: Fortress Press, 2015), 83.

20. Written by Jerry Leiber and Mike Stoller, "Is That All There Is?" won Peggy Lee a Grammy in 1969.

21. Michael Polanyi and Harry Prosch, *Meaning* (Chicago: University of Chicago Press, 1975), 177.

22. Polanyi and Prosch, *Meaning*, 173, 179.

23. Michael Polanyi, *Personal Knowledge: Towards a Post-Critical Philosophy* (London: Routledge, 1958).

24. Dorothy L. Sayers, *Creed or Chaos? Why Christians Must Choose Either Dogma or Disaster; Or, Why It Really Does Matter What You Believe* (Bedford, NH: Sophia Institute Press, 1995).

25. Steven Pinker, *Better Angels of Our Nature: Why Violence Has Declined* (New York: Viking, 2011) and *Enlightenment Now: The Case for Reason, Science, Humanism, and Progress* (New York: Penguin, 2018). However, Pinker is not despondent, as Sayers suggests about those who hold this worldview, but rather is happily optimistic.

26. George Marsden, *Twilight of the American Enlightenment: The 1950s and the Crisis of Liberal Belief* (Philadelphia: Basic Books, 2014).

27. See Alasdair MacIntyre, *After Virtue: A Study in Moral Theory*, 3rd ed. (Notre Dame, IN: University of Notre Dame, 2007).

28. Jonathan Rauch, "Let It Be," *Atlantic*, May 2003, www.theatlantic.com/magazine/archive/2003/05/let-it-be/302726.

29. Mathewes, "Toward a Theology of Joy," 82.

30. Andrew T. J. Kaethler, in the introduction to Georges Bernanos, *Joy* (Providence, RI: Cluny Media, 2020), viii.

31. Annie Dillard, *The Writing Life* (New York: Harper & Row, 1989; repr., New York: Harper Perennial, 2013), 68.

32. Buechner, *Longing for Home*, 108.

33. W. H. Gardner and N. H. MacKensie, eds., *The Poems of Gerard Manley Hopkins* (Oxford: Oxford University Press, 1967), 66.

34. Berger, *A Rumor of Angels*, 53–54. A similar argument is made by Alvin Plantinga in *Where the Conflict Really Lies: Science, Religion, and Naturalism* (Oxford: Oxford University Press, 2011), where he asserts that all scientific inquiry is founded on the principle of order in the universe, a view that is supported by religion but not naturalism.

Chapter 12

1. Pablo Picasso, "Picasso Speaks: A Statement by the Artist," *The Arts*, May 1923: 315.

2. C. S. Lewis, *The Weight of Glory, and Other Addresses* (New York: HarperCollins, 1949), 29.

3. C. S. Lewis, *The Last Battle (The Chronicles of Narnia, Book 7)* (New York: Harper Trophy, 2000), 196.

4. Charles Mathewes, "Toward a Theology of Joy," in *Joy and Human Flourishing: Essays on Theology, Culture, and the Good Life*, ed. Miroslav Volf and Justin E. Crisp (Minneapolis: Fortress Press, 2015), 82.

5. Richard John Neuhaus, *Death on a Friday Afternoon: Meditations on the Last Words of Jesus from the Cross* (New York: Basic Books, 2000), 39–40.

6. As quoted in Robert McAfee Brown, *Spirituality and Liberation: Overcoming the Great Fallacy* (Louisville, KY: Westminster John Knox, 1988), 136.

7. John Calvin, *Instruction in Faith (1537)*, trans. Paul T. Fuhrmann (Louisville, KY: Westminster John Knox, 1977), 55.

8. Arnold Benz, *The Future of the Universe: Chance, Chaos, God?* (Sacramento, CA: Continuum Press, 2002).

9. John Polkinghorne and Michael Welker, "Introduction: Science and Theology on the End of the World and the Ends of God," in *The End of the Universe and the Ends of God: Science and Theology on Eschatology (Theology for the 21st Century)*, ed. John Polkinghorne and Michael Welker (Harrisburg, PA: Trinity Press International, 2000), 7.

10. Tod Friend, "Silicon Valley's Quest to Live Forever," *New Yorker*, March 27, 2017, www.newyorker.com/magazine/2017/04/03/silicon -valleys-quest-to-live-forever.

11. Frederick Buechner, *The Longing for Home: Recollections and Reflections* (San Francisco: HarperSanFrancisco, 1996), 113.

12. J. R. R. Tolkien, "On Fairy-Stories," in *The Tolkien Reader* (New York: Ballantine Books, 1966), 86.

13. Letter 89, in *The Letters of J. R. R. Tolkien* (London: George Allen and Unwin, 1981).

14. Frederick Buechner, *Telling the Truth: The Gospel as Tragedy, Comedy, and Fairy Tale* (New York: Harper and Row, 1977), 98.

15. Words and music by Robert J. Stamps, © 1972 Dawn Treader Music.